THE
EVOLVING
SALES ENGINEER

UPDATED VERSION

EDWARD S. LEVINE

First published by Dog Ear Publishing
4010 W. 86th Street, Ste H
Indianapolis, IN 46268
www.dogearpublishing.net

ISBN: 978-1-4575-1312-1

This book is printed on acid-free paper.

Printed in the United States of America

This book is dedicated to the curious.

It was inspired and written for those
who believe that there is always
more to learn and who consistently and
proactively seek new ways of delivering
exceptional value to clients and colleagues.

TABLE OF CONTENTS

Introduction

*"I like talking to SEs because
they have something interesting to say."*
IT Director

Picture yourself standing at the ocean shore, feeling the cool water rushing in and out over your feet. One after the other, the waves magically appear and disappear. They change intensity, frequency and shape but never stop, they just keep coming. They are beneficial as well, creating new life forms and evolving the landscape with their unstoppable energy.

Waves of change continue to evolve the landscape for sales engineers as well. Expectations and demands on sales engineers (SEs) are changing as fast as the products they represent. These changes, like the ocean tide, are also beneficial. New technology means new needs for products, services, knowledge, knowledge transfer, technical assistance and complimentary products (i.e., new companies).

The goal of this book is to share with you strategic and tactical essentials that will contribute to your success, based on the need for change that SEs and their management teams now face. You will learn what it takes to be an *evolving* sales engineer, increasing your value to clients and internal team members.

My company has had the chance to work with many SE organizations and consistently hears about the growing need for flexible and independent SE teams. In fact, some level of consultative selling skills, which used to be on the wish list for hiring SE managers, has become the expected. The bar has been raised and it is incumbent on today's SE teams to develop the skills required to meet this challenge.

My organization has also interviewed many end users regarding the perceptions they hold of visiting SEs. They have shared stories, which you will read about later, that demonstrate outstanding techniques and other stories of good intentions gone awry. You will find that these real world scenarios provide excellent reinforcement of how, when applied properly, simple and well-timed techniques can redefine a relationship.

We have also had the pleasure of working with sales forces who count on their SEs for much of the "heavy lifting." A growing question in the marketplace is, *"What are the best ways to leverage our SEs' time?"* Organizations are struggling to find that right mix of when to deploy SEs in the sales cycle. We have heard from SEs who feel like *they are* the salesperson, being asked to control just about every aspect of the sale beyond high level relationship building and price negotiating. But isn't that the SEs' role? After all, we are in charge of pre-sales, right? This book will explore and define the SE's role and scope, considering all the variables that help the SE/account manager team maximize partnership performance.

THE EVOLUTION MARCHES ON

Historically, an SE's main job has been to deliver *technical messages* to *technical audiences*. To succeed as an evolving sales engineer you now need to:

- Be perceived as a technical expert and business partner
- Build relationships with multiple functions, including managerial and sometimes executive levels
- Fully understand the client's business model and organizational structure
- Connect technical features to business drivers and pain points
- Be more autonomous and self-sufficient
- Professionally and independently conduct discovery conversations and needs analyses
- Create and deliver persuasive presentations, often with little input from account managers (AMs)
- Plan and execute joint calls with AMs and other team members
- Speed up the sales cycle
- Help uncover opportunities for cross-selling and expansion within existing accounts

To better understand what changes are needed, think about SEs who you believe are top-performers and could serve as role models. What traits do these SEs possess that make them so special? In our workshops, we often hear answers including:

- Excellent communicators
- Able to connect technology to relevant customer needs
- Confident, enthusiastic presenters
- Able to maintain excellent relationships, particularly with AMs
- Great at asking the right question at the right time
- Flexible with change

Yes, extensive product knowledge will continue to be a requirement but, as you can see, the traits above have little to do with technical expertise. Instead, they are very personal and, unlike technology, difficult to exactly define or quantify. They are traits that some have a natural flare for or have learned through experience. Either way, they are true differentiators that every sales engineer has the potential to possess.

FORCES OF CHANGE

Change comes at us from all directions and at times certainly feels overwhelming. As an evolving sales engineer there are many unstoppable forces of change that necessitate the need for your evolution.

TIME PRESSURE

Today's accelerated pace has increased time pressures dramatically. Inventions such as cell phones and laptops that were supposed to relieve time pressures have had the opposite effect by merely raising the bar on productivity expectations. Because time is our scarcest resource, excellent time management skills are now a must for SEs. Sales engineers who have traditionally excelled in extensively analyzing problems and experimenting with solutions must now be far more sensitive to their time allocation choices. Delivering maximum ROI on time invested is now, more than ever, an important part of the evolving SE's skill set.

One time management example relates to how much information SEs choose to share with clients. How many times have you heard a sales engineer say something like, *"This is a little off topic but I thought you might find this next feature really interesting."* This is NOT a statement that you will hear from evolving sales engineers who understand the premium value that others place on their time. Separating the "need to know" from the "nice to know" is an important topic that will be dealt with later in the book.

Clients, AMs and other team members now feel the same time pressures as SEs. The ways that SEs interact with others should benefit these parties as well. Often, others will not speak up when they think that sales engineers are wasting their time. They'll be polite, attentive and then roll their eyes or complain to others later. Conversely, if sales engineers are succinct with their message and clearly respectful of the time needs of others (especially AMs) they will receive praise and positive reinforcement as others will seek to reinforce the SE's productive behaviors. This may come in the form of a simple comment like, *"Thanks for summarizing the proposal. I really didn't have the time to fully analyze it."* This kind of feedback lets sales engineers know that they are going in the right direction when it comes to relieving the time pressures that others are experiencing.

Advancements in Technology

If you are under 30, an answering machine is a Hollywood prop. Texting is quickly replacing email. Students frequently tell me that they do not listen to voicemail, instead they look at the number and, if recognized, they call it back.

For an SE, this built in obsolescence is a beautiful thing. It guarantees a never ending flow of new, emerging product and solutions that will require some level of pre-sales effort. Top performing SEs will almost certainly have many employment options as wave after wave of technical breakthroughs continue to reach our shores.

These rapid changes in technology are certainly affecting your company's product mix as well. Assuming your company is more than three years old, look at what your products and services are today vs. in the past. If your company is relatively new, what outdated competitor are you attempting to dethrone?

In addition to consistently updating your product knowledge, these changes in technology also mean that you need to be proficient at **communicating with clients through a variety of mediums**. These include: email, voicemail, face to face, social networking, web and video conferencing. Different rules of engagement apply to each. Evolving sales engineers need to learn and apply these rules in order to maximize their value, independent of what communication tool they are using. The pros and cons of each communication tool will be explored later in this book as well.

A GLOBAL MINDSET

As an evolving sales engineer you must now think and act globally— even in your own backyard. The volume of international and cross-cultural communications escalates at an unprecedented rate. As global satellite offices spring up and off-shoring success stories increase, your ability to adjust to a seemingly borderless world will directly impact your success.

Let's say, for example, that you are asked to present a product overview to a prospective client. You're expecting three attendees but Sam, the salesperson, was too busy to get you their names. He assured you that they are all in IT, and advised you to "just do the usual demo."

You enter the client's conference room to set up. It's a typical corporate facility—a rectangular dark wooden table, eight black leather chairs, a great view of downtown and plenty of air conditioning. You can smell the fresh food that they are setting up in the room next door. Food you know they will be offering you after your skillful presentation. Sam gave you no warning signs regarding this group. He is pretty good at letting you know when there may be trouble or something unusual, so you're not anticipating any issues. There will only be three attendees. This looks like it is going to be fun and easy!

After a run to the restroom to check your appearance, you return and the attendees are all present. They have filled out their name tents. Each of them is from a country other than yours, representing Europe, South America and Asia. What first felt like an easy assignment now has you in a bit of a panic. Experience has taught you that, while some cultural adjustments are useful, over-adjusting can create problems of its own. Plus, considering that attendees from three different countries are represented, how do you adjust to one without possibly losing or offending the others?

As these kinds of situations continue to occur it is helpful to have globally-proven techniques to fall back on and apply. The techniques you will read about in this book have been taught in North America, Latin America, The Middle East, Asia and Europe. To some extent, I have been surprised at how scalable the techniques are, regardless of location or cultural differences. How exactly you apply each will vary slightly by region, but be confident that they have been successfully introduced around the world.

INTERNAL EXPECTATIONS

In most companies that utilize sales engineers:
- Products and services are constantly evolving
- Client bases are large and fluid, regularly changing in size and definition
- Performance metrics for sales engineers change regularly
- Price and resource pressures usually mean spreading the SE team thinner

If you belong to a company that does not possess some or all of these traits, there probably is little pressure on you to change, evolve or redefine your role as an SE. But this does not mean that you can't or shouldn't evolve. In fact, by embracing this book's content you will differentiate yourself from your peers and are likely to find new doors opening and opportunities surfacing because of the new ways you will be perceived.

However, for most sales engineers these bullet points accurately describe their company's environment and, in one way or another, are related to sales challenges. It's good to remember that the first word in sales engineer is *"sales."* Because your efforts are inexorably tied to the sales effort, the most important internal expectations to be aware of (outside of your manager's) are those of your account managers.

The account manager owns the account.

You, along with consultants, product specialists, technical account managers, global account managers and others, are on the AM's team. AMs usually don't choose their SEs but SEs should think of themselves as working for their assigned AMs. You are there to help AMs drive revenue. Period. Account managers perceive a client as *their client* and expect to be treated as the owner of the account when it comes to strategic and critical decisions.

As controlling as this all may sound, AMs now actively seek to hand over as much control as possible to SEs who they can trust. The trend is for AMs to seek evolved SEs who can take on more of the traditional sales functions, freeing AMs to find new opportunities and expand within current accounts. SEs are increasingly being asked to independently:
- Build quality relationships
- Conduct needs analyses
- Uncover potential objections
- Define the competitive landscape

Account managers will seek out, appreciate, value and reward sales engineers who see themselves as more than just product experts. Impressing your account managers with your abilities beyond the technical should be one of your key goals. It will lead to more symbiotic partnerships and greater job satisfaction, based on mutual respect and trust.

COMPETITION

Competition comes from two different worlds. In the first world you are compared to your competitors' SEs.

How do you stack up against the SE the competition sends out to the field? Because most sales occurs when you are not there (internal client meetings, client discussions with the competition, etc.) you will rarely know the answer to this question. You will show up, interact, get a gut feel for your impact and move on, usually with no direct client feedback. Clients will generally be polite to you regarding your performance, "*Thank you. That was very informative.*" and certainly tight-lipped regarding the performance of your competitions' sales engineers. Win or lose the deal, you will rarely know how you actually compared to the competition, making it difficult to assess how much your personal contribution impacted the final decision.

The second world is you compared to all sales engineers in the market, including your own team's SEs. Depending on your company's success and your own career goals, you may someday be competing against these sales engineers for other internal or external jobs. If you aspire to increase your internal responsibilities or are seeking new employment options, then your evolutionary progress relative to all other SEs takes on even greater significance.

Top performing sales engineers are always evolving. Traditional sales engineers who feel no sense of urgency to change will see the gap between themselves and their peers continue to expand. They will not understand why they didn't get that new job or why they are always passed up for promotion. Many will play the blame game and become chronic victims. They will blame office politics or other external influences (*"I just don't think the boss likes me."*) when the truth is that they're being passed by evolving sales engineers—SEs who understand the demand for change and upgrade their skill sets to meet the challenge.

This Book's Focus

I have divided this book into three major sections:

1. **Sales Engineer Management**
2. **Strategic Thinking for Sales Engineers**
3. **Tactical Techniques for Sales Engineers**

The management section outlines critical tools for choosing, assessing and developing sales engineer teams. It is written for managers yet is included for all to see. Instead of writing a separate book for managers, I thought it would be important for SEs to see how managers are being encouraged to plan and act. SEs will gain important insight into how they are being evaluated, allowing them to make changes to best align with management goals and expectations. If you are a manager, this section will surely provide you with new techniques for developing high performance teams.

The strategic section will examine topics where thoughtful planning is required. This section will address big picture questions that are useful to consider, along with other thought-provoking, high-level issues. It will show you a process for "mapping" or analyzing an account to help you develop a game plan for engaging the client. It will also exam the world of office politics and provide keys to keeping account managers happy—two topics often marginalized or taken for granted. Most sales engineers receive little training in these strategic areas yet, when properly executed, these strategies can seriously impact sales performance.

The tactical section consists of interpersonal skills that can be immediately applied to actual customer interactions. I have compiled these based on more than 15 years of teaching and consulting experience with sales engineers, professional services teams, account managers and executives. Out of the lengthy list of behaviors to choose from, these stand out as some of the most important contributors to the evolving sales engineer's success. They are not sales gimmicks or clever scripts. Instead, they are proven techniques for interacting on a consultative, professional level.

WELCOME CHANGE

"Change is hard because people overestimate the value of what they have and underestimate the value of what they may gain by giving that up."

James Belasco and Ralph Stayer
Flight of the Buffalo (1994)

Welcoming change may be the most important mindset required for ensuring your long-term career success and emotional fulfillment. If you have been a sales engineer for a great length of time, you might understand and agree with this concept on a cerebral level, but *fully* welcoming change can still be quite challenging.

Change has always been a constant but the speed and brevity of change for sales engineers is at an all time high. Historically, SEs could sign on with a large company and almost be assured of job security as long as they knew their technology and didn't make any major mistakes. Change for SEs usually consisted of learning new products, which were introduced at a much slower rate than they are today.

The relatively high turnover rate for account managers contributed to the SEs' security as well. Because so many AMs were new, SEs had tremendous power over these AMs who were dependent on the SE's technical knowledge. Demand for the SE's time far outstripped supply, thereby raising the SE's value. It was not uncommon to hear stories about AMs *begging* SEs to help them with their accounts. While the turnover rate for AMs is still higher than for SEs, the speed of technology change has dampened this phenomenon as well. An SE who has been around for 90 days may have as much required knowledge as one who has been with the company for many years.

Most SEs are willing to *surrender* to change. Surrendering, however, is different than *welcoming*. The difference can best be found in the contrasting gut, emotional reactions that SEs experience when they are asked to do something out of their comfort zone. *Welcoming* SEs feel a heightened sense of energy, awareness and enthusiasm. When they are informed that current technologies or ways of doing business are no longer optimal, they perceive the change as an opportunity to enhance their value. Change is positive.

For surrendering SEs, change is painful. It is de-motivating and deflating. They struggle to overcome initial negative reactions and must talk themselves into accepting the inevitable. When change is required, welcoming SEs say *"Let's go!"*, surrendering SEs say *"Oh, no!"*

Surrendering SEs are easy to spot based on their verbal and nonverbal reactions, and obvious lack of enthusiasm when change is introduced. Others will sense their dissatisfaction and these SEs, unknowingly, will be perceived as inflexible, complacent or "old school." Team members will begin to dread communicating future changes to these SEs, expecting push-back and negativity. Exciting, higher-level projects, plus promotions and perks, will get channeled to the more change-welcoming SEs.

So how do you *sincerely* become an SE who welcomes change?

The first step to welcoming change is awareness.

Become aware of how much or little you welcome change. If you truly understand the constant need for change and are willing to let go of the comfortable present, be sure to demonstrate this attitude whenever possible. If you would rather not deal with constant change, then it is important to assess why you feel this way and start working on ways to overcome this counterproductive mindset.

One way to help your attitude towards change is to ponder its positive aspects. By focusing on the plus side, you may find increased motivation to be more welcoming.

Change:
- Creates opportunities for you and others
- Indicates that your management is open to fresh ideas
- Leads to discovering new tasks and activities that you might enjoy and excel in performing
- Increases your knowledge base and market value
- Increases your company's chances of survival and growth

Frequent and dramatic changes will continue to define your existence as a sales engineer. These changes will affect your company's products, its structure, the competition and what is expected of you, knowledge-wise and behaviorally.

****

The SE role continues to evolve and offer significant opportunities to those who are willing and able to meet the challenge. As the tides of change keep rolling up on your shore, this book will provide you with immediately applicable ideas and techniques to help you evolve as an SE or SE manager. There's a lot to explore together, so thank you for your support and let's get to it!

MANAGING THE EVOLVING SALES ENGINEER

INTRODUCTION

T his section is for managers, directors and executives interested in improving the consultative skills of their SE teams. Many of the ideas and techniques are the same as those used by my company, **Technically Speaking**, when consulting with SE organizations.

After careful consideration I have decided to include this section for all to see, even though it mainly focuses on management activities. Some of it may surprise your SEs, raising important questions and encouraging constructive discussion. Should your SEs read this section? Yes and here's why:

Managers of top performing SE organizations
encourage and model
an <u>open, consistent</u> flow of <u>accurate</u> information.

People want information, and lots of it, even if the information is not what they want to hear. A classic example of this occurs at airports daily.[1]

****

Imagine that you are waiting to board your flight when the gate agent makes this announcement:

"Ladies and gentlemen, we're sorry to inform you that our flight has been delayed. We're not sure what's going on yet. The plane is here, but the mechanics are telling us that it should be about 10 minutes before we can board. Thank you for your patience."

Okay, no panic. 10 minutes is no big deal and everyone gets back on their cell phones. Let's continue our story...

After 10 minutes there is no announcement.
After 15 minutes there is no announcement.
After 20 minutes there is no announcement.

How is everyone feeling now? People are probably getting irritated, many are approaching the gate agent to see what's going on and the mood is turning increasingly tense.

What if instead, after 10 minutes the gate agent made this announcement:

"Ladies and gentlemen, I just wanted to let you know that we have not been given any new information. We will give you updates every 10 minutes to let you know what, if anything, we've been told. Again, we're very sorry for this inconvenience and your next update will be at 12:15, based on the clock behind me."

What happens now? People get on their phones, get something to eat, read the newspaper or just relax.

They're not happy about the delay but by simply having the gate agent commit to an **open, consistent** flow of **accurate** information, anger and tension are diffused.

I once asked a gate agent (after waiting 20 minutes for an announcement) why she didn't keep us posted every few minutes? Her reply was, *"I have nothing new to tell you so why bother?"*

✳✳

The point of this story is that people want to be kept informed, regardless of the relative desirability of the information—SEs included. I understand that from a management level, not everything is appropriate for public consumption or scrutiny. However, even negative or disconcerting information (assuming it will not derail corporate initiatives) needs to be shared to maintain a trustful and healthy environment.

This section may contain just such information. SEs who read this may be surprised or even disagree with some of the ideas. However, if you are an SE, I would encourage you to objectively assess this section and understand that management is embracing and applying these strategies today.

THE ROLE OF THE SE MANAGER

The role of the SE manager is long overdue for evolution. Most SE managers today were previously SEs. That means that they probably entered the ranks as an SE at least 3-5 years ago. That was during a time when expectations for SEs were very different and more strictly defined. 90+% of your value rested with your *technical* expertise. If you could succeed with non-technical audiences or higher levels, that was great, but certainly not expected or required. The interview process that SEs went through focused almost entirely on technical know-how. Does this sound like your experience?

Coming from the SE ranks certainly has significant advantages when it comes to technical expertise and empathy. However, SE managers from purely technical backgrounds must now *drive* the changes required by the evolving SE. In many cases an SE's evolution and ultimate success is almost entirely dependent on his or her manager's coaching and development expertise.

The tricky part is that this is only possible when the SE managers are themselves proficient at the skills that they must model, coach to and reinforce. These are skills that they may have intuitively mastered yet have had little formal educational experience learning and, as a result, may find this knowledge challenging to transfer in a consistent and structured fashion.

This section will cover a number of topics that will help SE managers in their roles as hiring agents and coaches. They are:

- **Assessing current talent**
- **Charting competencies**
- **Choosing and developing talent**
- **Coaching**

****

In summary, this section will cover four of the most critical areas that today's SE managers need to master. This section is not designed to replace classroom or on-line training initiatives for management and leadership development. Managers are highly encouraged to enroll in such classes. However, the chapters that follow will provide SE managers with the fundamental behaviors and techniques that will lead to choosing the best people and then maximizing their potential.

(1) Out of 652 passenger complaints for the airlines industry (flight delays, baggage problems, ticketing, refunds, reservations, etc.) in October, 2008, 475 were categorized as *"Customer Service."* Source: US Department of Transportation, Air Travel Consumer Report, December, 2008.

Chapter 1

ASSESSING CURRENT TALENT

SE managers generally have a good feel for the talent levels of their teams. However, it can be a mistake to use broad-brush generalizations when attempting to describe or assess teams. Accurate assessments enable managers to identify who, specifically, are the best candidates for development initiatives, who require more direct feedback and coaching, and which development methodologies are most appropriate.

This chapter will focus on one option for assessing the team in order to build a more focused SE development strategy. This involves placing every SE into one of four groups, based on the organizational level that they have proven they can interact within successfully. In this approach, the highest level that SEs ascend to is called their "Success Zone." This is not their comfort zone. If you ask SEs which levels they are most comfortable interacting with, they will frequently respond with a higher level than that which they would truly succeed. It doesn't matter if they like presenting when there are VPs in the room. What matters is if they have the right persona, savvy and acumen to gain the respect of their audiences and move them to take the desired courses of action.

The process for assessing current talent works best when it involves those who:

· Have direct experience with the SE team members being assessed
· Have a stake in the results of contributing to the process
· Have enough management experience to know how to fairly and objectively conduct an assessment
· Do not have conflicting goals or priorities that would lead to skewed or self-serving responses

****

ASSESSMENT TABLE

Group	Success Zone	SE
#1	VP and above	
#2	Non-technical departments (HR, Marketing, Finance, Sales, etc.)	
#3	Technical Managers	
#4	Technical users (programmers, architects, etc.)	

This table is hierarchal. Each group is assumed to be competent at interacting with all the groups that fall below it in the table. This assumption works well with SEs but not with other titles. An account manager, for example, may be excellent interacting with VPs but is challenged by the technical staff. Because sales engineers have proven technical expertise, the hierarchal sequencing we are using is valid.

The number of groups and *Success Zone* titles in the table need to be tailored to fit your business model. Defining these zones often becomes a productive internal discussion and forces management to analyze and prioritize the SE teams and their focus. *Success Zone* titles will most likely be tied to how your SEs are organized. You may also have different tables for different SE categories. For example, you might have a group just calling on Enterprise accounts called **Enterprise SEs.** You would then have to change the *Success Zone* titles to match the Enterprise world. Titles may also change by industry or the size of the client's company. Interacting with the CEO, for example, may be unrealistic in larger accounts. This table uses a software company example but can easily be adapted to most industries. The *Success Zone* titles that were chosen for the example are the most commonly used when this analysis is conducted.

CATEGORIZE BY INDIVIDUALS

It may be tempting for SE managers to look at this table and give a snap judgment regarding where the bulk of their SEs fit in. However, a far more comprehensive and idea-provoking approach is for managers to categorize each of their SEs individually. This task is not terribly time consuming and will serve as an important mental exercise, encouraging managers to think about their SEs in this important context.

Each manager would place one mark for each of their respective SEs in one of the four boxes, representing their *Success Zone*. This information is then forwarded to one point of contact who would compile the data and produce a table that would reflect the cumulative totals representing all of the company's SE teams, as shown in the following example.

Group	Success Zone	SE
#1	VP and above	14
#2	Non-technical departments	23
#3	Technical Managers	32
#4	Technical users	38

TEAM SHAPE—PYRAMID, TREE, HOUSE OR FUNNEL?

Next, the SE managers would meet, analyze the data and decide what shape best reflects the talent level of the SE organization as a whole. The group numbers in the completed table correspond to the group numbers in the shapes that follow.

Option #1 - Pyramid

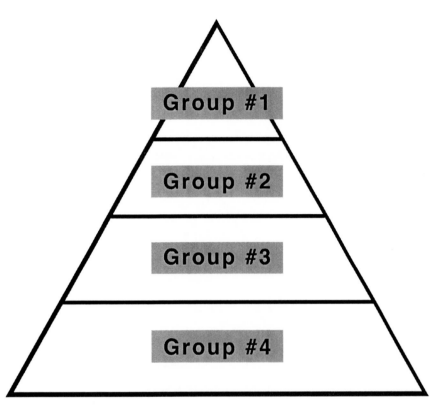

In this case, the bulk of the SEs hit their success ceiling interacting with technical users. We know this because the lowest polygon in the triangle had the most entries and requires the most space. This is often the case with a company that matured with a technical vs. marketing culture. The company has succeeded because of its technology and has experienced no compelling need to evolve its marketing approach or how SEs interact with its client base. Its products are also likely to have significant competitive advantages, allowing the company to continue to succeed with a primarily technical focus.

One current area that falls under this category is cloud computing. Companies that entered into this market early and are enjoying success can cruise on their vision with an extremely technical SE team and still enjoy impressive growth...for now. Past examples of companies that started in this manner include TIVO and RIM (Blackberry).

One permutation of this is the *"Tree"* effect.

Option #2 - Tree

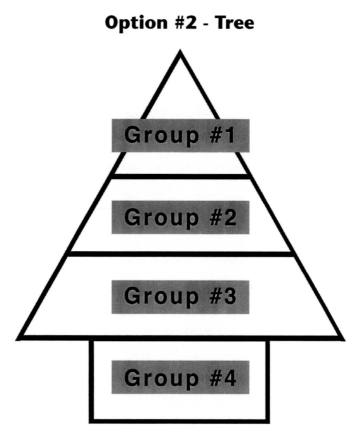

In this case, Group #3 represents the largest population, i.e. the bulk of the team maxes out their success zone with technical managers. There is a significant drop-off when it comes to VPs and above. This is the most common shape we see in SE organizations today and still indicates a fairly robust technical focus.

Option #3 - House

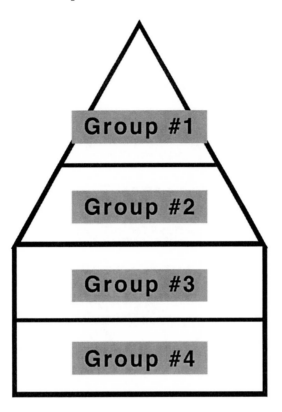

Similar to the tree shape, this would indicate that SEs are enjoying an equal amount of success with technical users, managers and non-technical departments. This represents a healthy balance between marketing and technical focuses.

Option #4 - Funnel

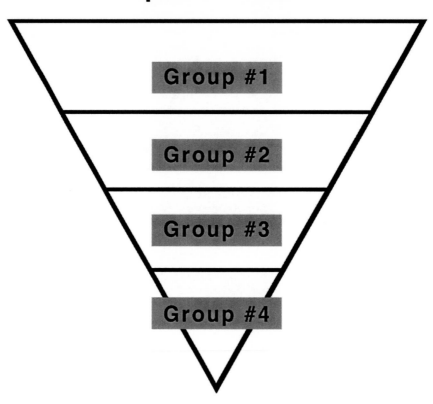

As unusual as it is desirable, the funnel shape indicates that the SEs are successful interacting at all levels. They are probably invited to high level meetings and their observations are sought after by clients and account managers. They can be counted on to come through in the most challenging of situations and AMs are likely to give them tremendous independence and latitude.

An SE team with this shape was probably recruited from top consulting firms or their organization has invested significantly in their consultative development. In addition, hiring criteria for SEs at this company likely emphasized interpersonal and consultative skills far more than may be industry typical.

Once a consensus has been reached on the shape of the SE organization, the management team should discuss next steps. I have facilitated many such meetings and find they are most productive when guided by five key questions:

- **What do we like and not like about our team's shape?**

- **What group # should be our top priority and what specific changes to that group need to occur?**

- **Which improvement option or combination of options should be considered and why?**
- **Training**
  - ☐ **One-on-one coaching**
  - ☐ **Mentoring program**
  - ☐ **Attrition**
  - ☐ **Active replacement**

- **Both ideally and realistically, what do we want the SE team's shape to look like one year from today?**

- **When would it make sense to meet again to reassess the team and its progress towards achieving the desired new shape?**

****

The pyramid, tree, house and funnel shapes are, of course, clean ideals. Rarely will the numbers be so pure that they exactly depict these shapes. But the goal here is not to create geometrically-correct diagrams. The goal is to create an accurate, graphic depiction of the current state of the company's SEs, allowing management to engage in data-driven dialogue regarding team direction and development.

Chapter 2

CHARTING COMPETENCIES

Another important step is the building of a competency matrix. This can be done in conjunction with or independent of the team shape activity from the previous chapter. SE managers should be directly involved in completing this exercise. It can potentially change the way people are hired, compensated, promoted or reallocated. Input needs to be elicited from the highest levels and Human Resources should also be kept in the loop. As a manager, you will find this activity to be an excellent investment of your time. It will force you to think about the specific skills that contribute most significantly to your team's success, and should be pursued and developed.

Some of this work is likely to have already been done at your company, so you may not need to reinvent the wheel. Unfortunately, existing competency matrixes are often designed by people with minimal sales engineering experience or little knowledge of the latest expectations being placed on SEs. They may also use templates from previous companies that lack current validity. Sometimes avoidance to update competencies is connected to how time consuming and complex the task can become. Unless their jobs are directly affected, few are eager to initiate this process unless required to do so.

It is, however, important to review existing work before reinventing the wheel. The previous attempts will usually contain ideas that you may not have considered or, at minimum, will act as excellent starting points for discussion and creation of the new competencies. In addition, huge changes in this area may confuse the field and send a message of management inconsistency. Leverage what has been done but have the courage to redefine expectations.

To assist in building your own matrix, it is helpful to contrast the traditional SE with the evolving SE. This table will give you context to help craft competencies based on your company's specific needs.

****

Traditional SE	Evolving SE
Hiring process consists of asking technical questions and candidate giving technical presentations	Hiring process consists of technical questions, presentations and behavioral interviewing questions designed to uncover personality traits and interpersonal skills
Once hired, only invited to technical training	Once hired, invited to technical and sales training
Minimal client contact during sales cycle before giving sales presentations	Extensive needs analysis and client contact before recommending solutions
Begins client communications with technical questions	Begins account communications by building rapport and focusing on strategic drivers
Interacts solely with technical layer to gather requirements before crafting proposal	Interacts with technical layer, lines of businesses, managers and executives before crafting proposal
Presents all product/service features that are considered competitive strengths	Presents minimal amount of data required to make business case

Traditional SE	Evolving SE
Focuses almost solely on client's technical needs	Focuses on technical needs, organizational issues, spheres of influence, office politics and decision process
Does not believe that appearance, presentation skills, or general image really make much difference in the final analysis	Believes that the personal image presented to clients plays a strong role in building relationships and impacting decisions
Is mainly *reactive* to needs of clients and account managers	Proactively drives sales conversation and uses assertiveness techniques to set expectations and ensure that SE needs are met as well
Is uncomfortable with, and avoids, tension and pressure	Understands that sales involves tension and pressure—maintains composure and control under these conditions

Below you find a sample portion of a competency matrix that Technically Speaking worked with an SE management team to develop. In this example, the required competencies were broken down into the following categories:

- **Technical Skills**
- **Client Management**
- **Interpersonal Skills**
- **Presentation Skills**
- **Meetings Management**
- **Strategic Thinking**
- **Self Management**

As you will see, there is some overlap. For example, Interpersonal Skills are clearly part of Meetings Management. The goal of identifying and prioritizing competencies allows for this overlap to occur. Whenever interpersonal skills are involved, overlap is bound to occur, so be careful not to get bogged down in attempting to include competencies that are mutually exclusive.

Details are given when the competency's definition is highly subjective. In the *Group* columns, a mark would be placed if the management team deems that the competency must be acceptably and effectively performed by that SE group. For purposes of this example, four groups are used and possess the same definitions as the four groups in the chart from the previous chapter, *Assessing Current Talent*.

Those groups were:
Group #1 – VP and above
Group #2 – Non-technical departments (HR, Marketing, Finance, Sales, etc.)
Group #3 – Technical managers
Group #4 – Technical users (programmers, architects, etc.)

Competency	Details	Group #1	Group #2	Group #3	Group #4
TECHNICAL SKILLS					
Programs in JAVA					
Programs in J2EE					
Debugs code					
Client Management					
Maps/understands organizational structure	Uncovers spheres of influence, lines of authority, decision making processes				
Understands access to funds					
Understands client's ROI and consequences related to project's success/failure					
Self-markets with executive assistants	Increases his/herperceived value to multiple departments				
Succeeds with executive accountants					
Delivers bad news					
Defends the company					
Deals with champions of other technologies					
Deals with inherited problems/attitudes					

Competency	Details	Group #1	Group #2	Group #3	Group #4
INTERPERSONAL SKILLS					
Manages conflict					
Appeals to different titles	Crafts/adjusts message based on the other party's title				
Maps/understands organizational structure	Uncovers spheres of influence, lines of authority, decision making processes				
Is assertive	"Pushes back" when believes he/she is right or has better options. Guards self-interest in ways taht are assertive vs. aggressive				
Builds relationships/ loyalty					
Negotiates effectively	Negotiates for resources, breaks deadlocks with give and take techniques and attitude				
Handles objections/ concerns					
Diffuses anger					
Reads/adjusts to individual styles	Adjusts to the other party's personality traits				
Says "No" when appropriate					

Competency	Details	Group #1	Group #2	Group #3	Group #4
PRESENTATION SKILLS					
Manages conflict					
Storyboards presentations	Tells a story that resonates and moves audience to desired actions				
Pre-assesses an audience					
Changes presentation techniques for smaller, less formal settings					
Sequences presentations effectively	Increases client urgency using the "gap" sequencing method				
Presents engagingly	Applies professional platform skills: eye contact, body movement, gestures, vocal tones, etc.				
Interacts effectively with visual aids	Properly uses laptop and white-boarding techniques				
Connects technology to client's business issues					

Competency	Details	Group #1	Group #2	Group #3	Group #4
MEETINGS MANAGEMENT					
Sets the stage, reviews, meeting goals, expectations and ground rules					
Facilitates brainstorming sessions					
Deals with "problem" meeting participants	Champions of other products, technical show-offs, etc.				
Plans and asks goal-oriented questions	Prepares questions based on the meeting's goals that create robust conversation				

Competency	Details	Group #1	Group #2	Group #3	Group #4
STRATEGIC THINKING					
Uncovers additional opportunities	Uses advanced questioning techniques to uncover opportunities while avoiding "sales pitches"				
Invents new ways of accomplishing the same task					
Learns the client's business and industry	Proactively learns enough detail to use client terminology and connect products to client issues and processes				
Connects technology to future business challenges					
Understands executive focus					
Builds multi-level relationships	Operations, Managerial, Executive				
Seeks to understand the bigger picture					
Drives conversations to higher business purposes	Connects technology to impact on stragetic initiatives				

Competency	Details	Group #1	Group #2	Group #3	Group #4
SELF MANAGEMENT					
Manages time to maximize productivity					
Copes with stress					
Balances work and life goals					

Once this table is complete, you would then create new charts detailing the competencies required for each group. The sample summary chart below shows what competencies were rated as required by an SE to be considered a *Group #3* SE.

Group #3 Competency Requirements Summary

SE: _____

Competencies	Meets Requirements
Technical Skills	
Programs in JAVA	☐
Programs in J2EE	☐
Client Management	
Understands client's consequences and paybacks related to the project	☐
Delivers bad news	☐
Defends the company	☐
Deals effectively with champions of other technologies	☐
Deals effectively with inherited problems/attitudes	☐
Meetings Management	
Sets the stage, reviews meeting goals, expectations, and ground rules	☐
Manages brainstorming sessions	☐
Deals with "problem" meeting participants	☐
Plans and asks goal-oriented questions	☐
Self Management	
Manages time to maximize productivity	☐
Handles stress professionally	☐
Balances work and personal lives acceptably	☐

As a manager, you would then complete a chart for each SE, based on the group number within which you believe the SE *should* reside. For example, if you believe that an SE should be succeeding with technical managers and below, you would complete a *Group #3* chart as shown above. You would then assess the SE based on your observations and experience, placing check marks in the *Meets Requirement* boxes.

THE ABLE/WILLING ANALYSIS

At this point you will know what, if any, required competencies your SEs are lacking to be fully qualified for the group numbers you have chosen for them. An easy, time-efficient next step is to apply the able/willing analysis. This will help you decide what next steps are most appropriate to facilitate their growth. While you may already be aware of this approach, in a world of complex processes it's easy to forget the power of this straight forward technique.

The able/willing analysis will act as your compass. It will tell you the direction in which you need to aim your efforts. The exact route you take and how you get there will require a different set of skills but at least the able/willing analysis will give you the confidence to know that you are starting off in the right direction before investing valuable time and resources.

Able = They have the skills needed to perform the competency.
Willing = They are interested in, and motivated to perform the competency.

1. If the SE is Able but Not Willing?

The sales engineer has the talent and knowledge to perform the competency but either doesn't want to, or sees no compelling reason to improve in the competency being considered. You have a motivation issue on your hands.

2. If the SE is Willing but Not Able?

The sales engineer has desire and interest in performing the competency but lacks the necessary skills or knowledge to do so at the required level. You have an issue with skills training.

3. If the SE is Not Able and Not Willing?

The sales engineer lacks motivation to improve in the competency and lacks the necessary skills or knowledge to do so. You have a compound issue and must assess the SE's ability to make meaningful contributions to the team in the future.

Sometimes all it takes are focused conversations with your SEs to conduct the able/willing analysis. Ask why they feel that they are deficient in the competencies not checked? Ask if they believe they need more training in these areas? Elicit their input as to what they believe would help them be more proficient at the competencies, and gauge their interest level in pursuing improvement in these areas.

If you believe an SE's reasons are more related to *not able* than *not willing* on a competency, you have easier options. These include:
- Enroll the SE in a class that focuses on the competency
- Recommend relevant books or other training resources
- Assign a role-model/mentor for the SE to watch performing the competency

- Offer to role-play in a safe environment so that the SE can practice and improve

The issue of *not willing* tends to be more challenging. In this situation:
- Seek to understand the SE's lack of motivation
- Share long term benefits of improvement
- Share possible consequences of not improving
- Highlight how proficiency has benefited other SEs
- Include support signals (*"I know you can do this," "I'll be here to help you in any ways you need," etc.*)

Whether the issue is one of able or willing, I would encourage you to:

Give your SEs every chance to succeed.

As a manager you should feel a sense of obligation to do everything in your power to help your SEs succeed before passing final judgments. This can mean providing them with the required tools for the job (able) or giving whatever attention, motivation or support (willing) the individual may require. By making their success your goal, you will learn your SEs' true potential and be able to make far more objective and fair decisions regarding their abilities. Many underperformers have blossomed into top performers simply because their managers were motivated to conduct the able/willing analysis, leading to unique, accurate and personalized development options.

****

Example

Ron, an SE manager I was working with, told me that he just couldn't get one of his SEs, Bill, to stop getting dragged into irrelevant technical discussions during presentations. An attendee might ask an off-topic question but instead of tabling the question for later, Bill would invariably tangent off into a lengthy explanation. The only people in the audience who weren't bored or irritated were the one asking the question and Bill.

Ron went on to say that he had told Bill many times to stop doing this but to no avail. Bill would say that he knew that this was a problem but could not seem to stop himself. Every question seemed fairly relevant to him and he didn't want to offend audience members by not answering their questions. I asked Ron whether he thought this was an *able* or *willing* issue. Ron, correctly I believe, thought it was an *able* issue. Bill had stated that he agreed with the problem and wanted to change, so motivation was not the issue. The focus of future coaching sessions needed to be on *how* to improve vs. *why* improvement was necessary or beneficial.

This simple discussion seemed very helpful for Ron. We developed options that focused on increasing Bill's ability to improve. Two ideas ended up helping Bill out tremendously. First, Ron had Bill play like he was an audience member while Ron presented. He told Bill to keep interrupting him and try to drag him off into tangents. Bill was able to observe how Ron consistently avoided the temptation and politely pulled the conversation back to the topic at hand. Next, Ron brought two other SEs into the room and had Bill present. This time the audience did the same thing to Bill, trying to entice him into his usual pattern of behavior.

These practice sessions were brief yet had enormous impact because the focus was on the **able** side of the equation. By allowing Bill to observe proper techniques from the customer's point of view and then role-play as an SE, his improvement in the field was immediate. Ron has told me that now when he recognizes a competency deficiency, his first reaction is to conduct an able/willing analysis.

Building competency matrixes is an important step in assessing and growing your team. It will provide you with specific ideas on what is required to succeed, based on how you group your sales engineers. It will provide jump off points for rich discussions regarding career growth and opportunities. Once you've charted competencies and conducted an able/willing analysis, you're ready to move on to developing your talent, which is explored in our next chapter.

Chapter 3

CHOOSING AND DEVELOPING TALENT

I have experienced interactions with managers and executives who, in frustration, deliver statements such as, *"We need to start over with that SE team."* I'm sure this feels empowering to say but it gives the illusion that dissatisfaction with an SE team is a problem that can be solved with a simple, broad brush solution. It also ignores the potential within the team that the company (or manager) has not explored.

These types of comments are usually not destructive and simply looked on as a venting of frustration. Other managers and executives who hear such comments usually do not take them seriously. These outbursts can, however, have a boomerang effect, making the one who offered the remark appear emotional and over-reactive. People tend to distrust leaders who give quick, emotional responses, while respecting those who take time to analyze difficult situations and offer plausible, logical options—even if those options cause organizational pain or take more time to enact.

58

But mismatches do exist. There will be SEs who are not able to meet the changing expectations being asked of them. When they realize that the job description they signed up for has changed, and if management is clearly communicating future requirements, these SEs may already be thinking about moving on, without requiring further conversations.

It is an important part of your work to observe when SEs are doubting their ability to meet future expectations or lack motivation to evolve. Let's say, for example, that you have an SE on your team, Serge, who you doubt will be able to become more "consultative" as required. You call Serge into your office and tell him that you would like him to go to training on interpersonal and presentation skills. This training will take him out of the field for about one week. It will include role-playing and videotaping of his presentation skills.

Watch Serge's initial non-verbal reaction to your training recommendation. Let's say that you perceive an immediately negative non-verbal response. Even if he follows up his non-verbal reaction with some form of enthusiasm, the negative reaction probably revealed some true, underlying feelings. Did Serge appear irritated? Insulted? Excited? Defeated? Appreciated?
Your nonverbal observations should be given a great deal of weight.

If you conclude that an SE is not capable of meeting the required expectations, action should soon follow. But before taking decisive steps, consider that reallocating him or her may:

THE EVOLVING SALES ENGINEER

- Damage team morale, unless the reasons for your actions are apparent or communicated to the team
- Undermine trust, particularly if the decision is a surprise to the SE and the team.
- Upset customers who like the SE
- Upset account managers who enjoy working with the SE
- Increase the work load on other SEs on the team
- Make it look like the decision to hire the SE was a bad initial management decision
- Result in being an expensive option. The cost of finding, hiring and training new employees is generally two to three times the cost of their annual salary

CHOOSING NEW TALENT

When it comes to choosing new talent, making great choices is extremely challenging. Candidate's today are better rehearsed than ever for interviews, having stock answers at the ready for just about every question tossed their way. Plus, litigious-sensitive HR departments will almost never give referral insight to inquiring companies. Any inquiries into personal attributes are rebuffed. Dates of previous employment are just about all recruiters can confirm, leaving the burden of subjective analysis completely up to the hiring committee and you, the SE manager.

One area of focus should be the crafting of truly revealing questions to ask candidates during the interviewing process. While this chapter cannot replace professional interviewing skills training, some general guidelines are important to know and are included here.

Being selective has its obvious benefits. A counter-vailing force is that, according to The Computer Research Association, 2005, nationwide in the U.S. the number of newly declared computer science majors decreased 39 per-cent from fall 2000 to fall 2004, from 16,000 to about 10,000 declared majors. Demand for talent is up yet the domestic talent pool is shrinking. This certainly helps to explain and understand the influx of talent into the U.S. from countries including Russian, India and China.

Material to this discussion is how SEs are educated. Most SEs have a degree in Computer Science. Curriculum for typical Computer Science degrees are shown below.

This one is from Northeastern Technical University, USA, 2004 curriculum.

CIS Core Requirements

COP 3502	Introduction to Computer Science	(3 credits)
COP 3330	Object-Oriented Programming	(3 credits)
COP 3331	Object-Oriented Analysis and Design	(3 credits)
COP 4601	Operating Systems & Concurrent Programming	(3 credits)
COP 4530	Data Structures, Algorithms & Generic Programming	(3 credits)
COP 4531	Complexity & Analysis of Data Structures & Algorithms	(3 credits)
COP 4710	Theory and Structure of Databases	(3 credits)
COP 3101	Computer Organization	(3 credits)
4000-level CIS electives (e.g., CIS 4601)		(9 credits)
Programming language course not covered in the above courses		(3 credits)

This next curriculum is for Level 1, Computer Science majors from the University of Hong Kong, 2006

One of the following combinations (6 credits):		
Major - Computer Science		
COP 4020	Programming Languages	(3 credits)
COT 4420	Theory of Computation	(3 credits)
OR		
Major - Software Engineering		
CEN 4010	Software Engineering Principles & Practice	(3 credits)
COT 4425	Formal Methods in Software Engineering	(3 credits)
	Sub-total	**42 credits**
Math/Science/Speech Courses		
MAC 2311	Calculus I	(4 credits)
MAC 2312	Calculus II	(4 credits)
MAD 2104	Discrete Mathematics I	(3 credits)
MAD 3105	Discrete Mathematics II	(3 credits)
STA 3032	Probability & Statistics for Sciences & Engineering	(5 credits)
SPC 2600	Public Speaking	(3 credits)
PHY 2048c	General Physics A (calculus-based)	(5 credits)
PHY 2049c	General Physics B (calculus-based)	(5 credits)
Science Electives for Science Majors - other than physics		(3 credits)
Sub-total		**32 credits**
Total Computer and Information Science Required Hours		**74 credits**

CSIS1117A	Computer Programming (Double, BioInf & CogSc) - Class 1
CSIS1117B	Computer Programming (ActSc & Sc) - Class 2
CSIS1117C	Computer Programming (CS & CS) - Class 3
CSIS1117D	Computer Programming (Minor & retakers)
CSIS1118A	Mathematical Foundations of Computer Science (taught with CSIS 1501)
CSIS1118B	Mathematical Foundations of Computer Science (CE & retakers)
CSIS1119A	Introduction to Data Structures and Algorithms (CS, CE, CogSc & Minor)
CSIS1119B	Introduction to Data Structures and Algorithms (Double, BioInf, CogSc & Minor)
CSIS1119X	Machine Organization and Assembly Language Programming
CSIS1120	Machine Organization and Assembly Language Programming
CSIS1410	Industrial Training (Summer 2005) Industrial Training (Summer 2006)
CSIS1411	Workshop Training
CSIS1412	Engineering Mathematics
CSIS1501	Foundations of Biocomputing (BioInf only) (taught with CSIS1118A)

Great education, but what's missing? Based on the evolving expectations detailed in this book, quite a bit is missing. If those experiencing these curriculums are planning on becoming SEs, or fate intervenes and they evolve into the role, there will be many gaps in their required skills. The above merely satisfy the old "price of admission" for holding a technical position.

Here are the areas of study that would round out individuals and prepare them far more comprehensively for their roles as evolving SEs. Imagine if, as part of a computer science degree, students were required to take classes such as:

- Finance – How money is allocated and budgets as determined by IT.
- Psychology – How to satisfy the business and personal needs of clients and team members.
- Executive Priorities – Learn about the focus of higher levels (VPs, Directors of IT, CIOs, CEOs, etc.) and how to interact with a variety of executive titles.
- Technical Presentation Skills[1] – How to organize a technical presentation for maximum impact, design visual elements and exude confidence when formally presenting.
- Marketing – How to customize and deliver a focused message that resonates with clients.
- Organizational Structures and Behaviors – Gain an understanding of corporate structures and strategies for maximizing productivity and increasing cross-functionally. Learn to negotiate with those over whom you have no direct power or authority.

(1) A large percentage of an SE's work involves presenting to clients yet none of the curriculums shown earlier offer a single Public Speaking class.

These are not areas that naturally interest Computer Science majors and so are unlikely to garner attention. But it would be interesting to gauge reactions if some of these classes were required. If this curriculum was promoted by a progressive university, it would certainly be seen as a differentiator, resulting in major advantages for students when seeking professional work that involves customer interactions. Graduates would be at an advantage over their technology-only focused competition in the job market; positive word of mouth would spread and the pioneering university would probably see increased enrollment in their evolved curriculum.

Until higher education sees greater value in exposing students to these types of classes, it will continue to produce technically astute graduates who are alarmingly deficient in consultative, interpersonal skills. As a result, SE hiring committees must anticipate and expect younger candidates to come to them with little or no interpersonal skills training. Interpersonal effectiveness in a business setting will be almost impossible to predict. Recruiters will continue to count on their "gut feeling" regarding how effective a candidate will perform in the field.

INTERVIEWING IDEAS

In Technically Speaking's *Interviewing Essentials* workshop, one of the key sections deals with asking *behavioral* questions. During an interview, managers should include questions that reveal the person's interpersonal skills in addition to the standard technical questions. These behavioral questions are designed to uncover how the candidate reacted in past job-related situations. Most applicants are likely to repeat behaviors from previous jobs when confronted with new, yet similar situations.

The #1 predictor of future behavior is past behavior.

Behavioral questions are amongst the toughest types to answer because they force the other party to reveal much about themselves, in the moment. These questions should be related to the competencies that you earlier identified as required to succeed at the group level for which the candidate is being considered. So, for example, let's say that you have identified the following competencies as required by a *Group #3* SE:

- **Deals effectively with "problem" meeting participants**
- **Negotiates skillfully**
- **Connects technology to business issues**

Based on these, the SE manager would craft behavioral-based questions to learn about the candidate's skill levels in these competencies.

For example:

- **Deals effectively with "problem" meeting participants**
  "Tell me about a time when you had a problem with someone at a meeting you were leading. What was he or she doing and what did you do to remedy the situation?"
- **Negotiates skillfully**
  "Think of a situation when you had to get something from someone you had no power or authority over and who was not being very helpful. How did you negotiate with him or her to get your needs met?"
- **Connects technology to business issues**
  "Please give me an example of a recent presentation you gave where you were able to connect your technology directly to the client's business needs."

Here are two interviewing bonus tips from our *Interviewing Essentials* program:

1. Use silence

Don't settle for answers like, *"I can't think of an example when I had conflict with someone."* Instead, be positive and encourage them to give a full response:

"That's okay, Jan. We all have occasional conflicts in the sales arena. Please, take your time and come up with an example. I'll wait."

Stop talking at that point and let them think. Nine out of ten times they will give you a revealing response. This also sends the message that you are expecting complete, thoughtful answers to the rest of your questions.

2. Walk candidates to their cars

When candidates leave your office they psychologically shift gears and, on a subconscious level, believe that the interview is over. Many a manager has been surprised at what candidates reveal when they drop their defenses at this point. It can also be interesting to see their cars! Candidates who brag about their sense of responsibility and have piles of parking tickets on the front seat may not be telling you the whole story. Bumper stickers can also reveal quite a bit about the candidate. Do you really want your SE pulling up to a customer's office with Jolly Roger skull and cross bone stickers covering the back bumper!

DEVELOPMENT OPTIONS

Let's assume that the interviews are over, the team is complete and you have charted competencies. The next logical step would be to decide how to increase the competency levels for those in need. This section will outline development options and offer guidelines for making the best choices. One of the important choices is whether to use internal resources or to go external and find vendors who specialize in the skill development areas specific to the needs of your SEs.

Here is a table contrasting the pros and cons of the most common options.

Skill Development Choice	Pluses	Minuses
Training conducted by internal staff	Excellent for company-specific topics such as technical training, performance management systems, etc. Relatively inexpensive Class size not an issue Total control over content and delivery	Loss of outside perspective Possibility of facilitators having underlying, political agendas Over-familiarity with facilitator (same person teaching many courses, leading to dampened participant enthusiasm) Lack of facilitator credibility (a negotiation consultant teaching a negotiation class vs. an internal "jack of all trades" facilitator who has been certified on a negotiation course)

Most of the competencies that the evolving SE will need to focus on are in the interpersonal skills category. Because of this, there is a good chance that your company will partner with an external training vendor who has proven expertise and a unique curriculum. SE managers should be heavily involved in interviewing and assessing external training partners if this path is chosen. Often vendor choices are made by internal education departments who have little or no SE field experience. These departments do have excellent contacts and knowledge that need to be respected and leveraged, however, the SE management team should be the final judge in deciding which vendor offers the most time-efficient and on-target solution. This is a good way to ensure that expectations are clearly communicated to the new training partner and to build buy-in from the management team as a result of its involvement.

The size of the training company is another criterion that needs to be considered. There are two main advantages of working with a large training company:
1. They can deliver many classes simultaneously.
2. Their products can be bought in volume, off the shelf and ready to go.

The disadvantages of a large company include:
- Customizing a specific program is relatively expensive
- Including components from other courses they offer (a "menu" approach) is usually not an option
- Large facilitator pools can lead to a lack of facilitation consistency

- Programs are less frequently updated, possibly leading to outdated terms and techniques

Customizing in particular merits a warning. Be wary of training companies that claim to customize their programs at no additional charge. Often this equates to plugging the client company's name into predetermined spots in the binder and including a few presentation slides that contain information gathered during the sales process.

True customizing will involve extensive changes to the binder, planning forms and other collateral materials. It will also include a significant investment of time on the part of the facilitator to learn your business and then leverage this knowledge during the training sessions by connecting course content to company-specific issues.

If your company needs numerous, simultaneous classes and the content of the "off the shelf" program meets your needs, a larger company is a solid choice. However, if your company and you would like to tailor a program to your company's specific needs, with lower development costs, a smaller training company has the edge.

How Training Succeeds

The quality of a program's content and the expertise of the facilitator are obvious factors that impact a workshop's success. But delivering an outstanding class is not enough to ensure retention and accomplish long-term development goals. Assuming that the session itself was successful:

The number one variable in determining the long-term impact of a training initiative is the amount of management reinforcement that follows.

One of the greatest frustrations in the Training and Development industry is the lack of managerial involvement in the post-workshop process. Often participants' managers either:

- Don't attend the training and never learn what was taught
- Take the training but conduct no post-workshop reinforcement activities

The results are predictable. Many of the key learning points begin to fade and ideas that were enthusiastically accepted in class become distant, unapplied memories.

When managers reinforce the program they:

- Dramatically increase the long term retention and application of the learning points
- Send a clear message to their SEs that this training was important and they expect the SEs to take it seriously

Most managers agree that reinforcement should be part of the training and development process, but what we often hear them say is that they don't have enough time for this activity. While time is always of the essence, if reinforcement is considered a top priority it usually makes it on their agendas. For example, if managers were told that in order to receive their bonuses they must conduct one-on-one reinforcement sessions with SEs after every communications course, the sessions would surely occur. It really is a matter of choice, not time.

As an SE, SE manager or executive, remember:

You vote with your time
and your people are watching!

If you devote time to reinforcing a training session, your team notices and will attach a higher value to the program. If you never allude to content from the program when interacting with your team, the training is perceived as low priority and may even be viewed as just a perk that management felt forced or obligated to offer.

One of the keys to increasing management reinforcement is to make it as easy and time-efficient for the managers as possible. One successful approach which we use at Technically Speaking is to create a *Management Reinforcement Process* document that is sent to each sponsoring manager before a workshop. The heart of the document is a series of coaching questions that managers are expected to ask workshop participants after the program. The beauty of this is that all the hard work has been done by us. All the manager has to do is read the questions and assess the SE's responses.

One byproduct of this approach is the effect the reinforcement process has on managers who cannot attend the actual sessions. What frequently happens is that by just reading the reinforcement questions the manager's interest in the program's content is piqued. They will often be curious about some of the terminology in the questions and how correct answers should be presented. They will often pick up the program binder and cruise through it based on their curiosity and the fact that they don't want to be embarrassed because of their own lack of expertise.

COMPENSATION

Technically Speaking surveyed 14 SE Executives in 2011 to learn more about SE compensation. The results were gathered and distributed anonymously. I thought you would be interested in our findings, which are included next.

_____

1. How much, if any, do you vary compensation by geography (indexing)?

While some indicated a high degree of sensitivity to geographic considerations (*"We adjust quite a bit based on cost-of-living. Our people in New York are paid more than other areas."*), others showed smaller adjustments (*"We adjust, but very little within a geography such as US or within a European country."*).

Intentionally or not, those who offer less geographic variations may be setting the stage for more negotiation opportunities when candidates request geographic compensation that is not part of the standard package. This approach could save the company money by not initially paying more for higher cost of living areas.

In a down economy, such as what we've witnessed since 2010, candidates may be reticent to attempt to negotiate for more and the strategy may succeed. One downside to having multiple negotiations for more expensive areas is that it brings into play all the HR and morale complications of having a range of agreements for SEs within the same region.

Conversely, by having minimum geographic variations, the company runs the risk of overpaying for lower cost of living areas. Is it really wise to pay an SE working in Houston close to the same base as someone in San Francisco?

Mentioned as more significantly impacting pay than geography is the skill level of the SE. As supply fluctuates, this issue clearly expands and contracts. Depending on the skill being sought, finding the right match presents quite a challenge.

For example, when surveyed on competency needs, some of our clients have recently mentioned their desire to find SEs with proven track records in succeeding with higher levels (IT Director and above). This generally requires an SE with at least 8-10 years of experience. These SEs will negotiate for higher pay and are less likely to be open to relocating.

Another desirable competency mentioned was finding SEs with significant vertical experience (Telco, Financial, etc.). These SEs are usually already employed and will require attractive packages to motivate a change. More generic categories, such as Enterprise SE, do not seem to require much additional compensation and are more available.

Federal teams are almost a category unto themselves. One mistake we've noticed is that some companies do not understand the Federal world enough to choose appropriate SEs. Often they will transfer an SE into the Federal group based on a technical match. If, for example, the SE will be calling on the DOD, a strong emphasis should be placed on some military experience. He/she also needs appropriate security clearances in place before attempting to contact the client.

2. How do you structure commission or bonuses based on team (AM and SE) revenue?

First, one of our respondents mentioned that there are labor laws outside of the US that can impact how commission is distributed. For legal reasons, I will not give details in this report but this is certainly worth confirming with HR.

There was consistency in how commission is dealt with outside of the US. In EMEA and APAC where SEs may have a whole country to cover, their commission is geo-centric and based on regional revenue. For strategic and named account SEs, 100% direct commissions is the standard.

In the US, direct commission is the most common choice. For accountability and motivation this was mentioned as the desirable structure.

For most geographic locations, SEs should expect to make about 20-30% of their base in commissions.

**3. What percentage of SE compensation typically ends up being a result of
these bonuses?**

SEs, like their account managers, have a wide range of realized commissions. The key variable here seems to be the number of accounts they support. SEs with one, named account, in a way "own one stock," while SEs covering numerous accounts have a "mutual fund portfolio," with lower home run potential but spread risk.

Feedback was given that some SEs make 100% of their salary in commission. These are almost always SEs associated with a named account that makes a large purchase, resulting in a windfall for the SE. However, the average response range was 25-35%, which is in alignment with the previously mentioned range on how SE compensation is structured.

This is pretty consistent around the world. For example, we recently saw ads for Senior SEs in London and Munich and that offered the following:

Munich
    "Salary: Circa 60,000 - 75,000 plus 13,000 - 18, 000 commissions."
London
    "Salary: £55k - £65k pa + £70-80K OTE + Benefits"

4. What is the average base salary for an SE in 2011?

The responses set a pretty consistent average at $120,000, with slight variations for skill level and the fore mentioned geographic indexing. FYI, in the US, according to Indeed.com, this represents a 12% increase from January 2010.

Survey Summary

In summary, the only major differences in the survey answers related to geographic indexing. Other categories, such as percentage of commission to base, and base pay received similar responses. It also seems clear that specialized SEs (executive level skilled or vertically experienced) are increasingly harder to find and more expensive. Finally, salaries have crept up but are still below pre-recession (2009) levels.

GOOD NEWS FOR EMPLOYERS

The Computing Research Association collected enrollment data in fall 2008. The computer science and computer engineering departments of 192 Ph.D.-granting universities participated in the survey. The findings indicate that the pool for well educated technical talent is on the rise. Not all of these graduates will have the variety of skills needed to be a top-performing SE, but the numbers are encouraging.

The findings included:

- Total enrollment by majors and pre-majors in computer science was up 6.2 percent per department over 2007. If only majors are considered, the increase is 8.1 percent. This is the first time total enrollment increased in six years.

- The average number of new students per department majoring in computer science is up 9.5 percent over 2007. Computer science departments are replenishing the freshman and sophomore ranks with larger groups than they are graduating as seniors. Computer science graduation rates should increase in two to four years as these new students graduate.

- Bachelor's degree graduation production in computer science was down 10 percent in 2008, compared to a nearly 20 percent decline in 2007. This is the smallest graduating computer science class in ten years.

- Total Ph.D. graduation production among responding departments grew to 1,877. This represents a 5.7 percent increase over 2007.

✳✳✳

This chapter has included practical tips for choosing team members and developing your team's talent. Because so much of what SE's do today requires autonomy and trust, SE managers must work diligently to make wise hiring decisions and then offer development options that maximize each team member's potential. SE managers must also remember that their involvement in post-training reinforcement is the most important contributing factor in the long-term retention and application of developmental initiatives.

Chapter 4

COACHING

Coaching is considered to be the quickest, most powerful and personal development choice for helping an SE achieve lasting change. Most SE managers are trained in general management skills and how to give feedback but few know what is involved in forging a true coaching relationship. While there is some overlap between these activities, coaching has many unique and distinct traits.

Coaching is about creating a supportive climate and an on-going process for developing an individual. It is the simultaneous focus on professional development and task improvement compared to simply giving feedback about specific task improvement.

Coaching opportunities include assisting individuals to:
- Develop professionally
- Enhance work quality
- Find new, better ways of accomplishing tasks
- Interact more effectively with peers and cross-functionally
- Handle challenging, pressure situations

Coaching should be a mutually beneficial and positive experience. Most successful executives, like successful athletes, use coaching regularly to help polish their skills and overcome external and personal obstacles. It is a very powerful tool to create lasting change. Particularly if SEs feel challenged or overwhelmed with rising expectations, coaching will become an increasingly important option for helping them succeed. Coaching will also increase team members' appreciation of their manager's personal commitment to their success.

Coaching should be:
- An ongoing process
- A way to enhance relationships
- A way to improve SE retention
- A positive growth experience for the coach and the SE
- A morale booster

Coaching should *not* be:
- A onetime event
- A "nice" way to discipline team members
- A sneaky way to delegate
- A deep, personal, psychological journey

✼✼✼

How would you feel if your manager opened a coaching session as follows?

"Bobby, thanks for coming in today. I wanted to give you some coaching tips that I think you'll really enjoy. Feel free to jump in at any time because I'd like this to be interactive. Okay? Great.

First, you obviously know the product and that's great. The problem I'm seeing is that you're not connecting any of our features to what's really important to the client. For example, when you started talking about how our products are standards based, I would have talked about how important this was to a growing company. And let me tell you, I've done a lot of presentations where just by saying something like, that everyone could see that I understood their current situation. Looking back, that's one of the main reasons that I think we got the Unitech Bank's business. I did the final presentation and everybody was impressed. Last year they were our most profitable customer.

Next, you really need to work on how you handle questions. Half the time I couldn't hear what the question was, so be sure to repeat questions for the group. Your eye contact was good at the beginning and end but in the middle you only looked at James. I would have looked more at Tim and Susan. Remember, they're making the final call here.

Also, I couldn't help but notice that you kept talking to the white board. You probably don't know how to avoid that so here's what I usually do ..."

****

How is this coach doing so far? How do you think the SE is feeling? While the coach's heart and intentions seem to be in the right place, the coach is basically presenting a laundry list of improvement notes. The SE is being pummeled with negatives. In addition, the coach keeps bringing personal techniques into the mix instead of giving the SE a chance to come up with options or solutions. Many managers "coach" their people in a similar fashion. They think that because the SE sits quietly, takes notes and then thanks them afterwards, it was a good coaching session.

The example above does not qualify as a coaching session. Let's take a closer look at the origins of coaching, how it differs from feedback and how to conduct a productive coaching session.

THE ORIGINS OF COACHING

We begin our coaching classes by asking the following:

"Where do you think the term 'coach' comes from?"

The predictable responses are sports related—soccer coach, football coach, baseball coach, etc. We all had coaches in school. Some teachers were just called "Coach." The term "coach," however, actually originated many years ago, when the most common mode of transportation was a horse-drawn carriage, or **coach**.

A "coach" is a vehicle that takes you from one place to the next.

Your job as a manager is to be the vehicle that takes your SEs from one place to the next in terms of their professional development.

FEEDBACK VS. COACHING

It is important to understand the differences between giving feedback and coaching. Many managers believe that they are basically the same. Giving feedback is usually focused on telling an individual how they accomplished a specific task (i.e. gave a presentation, interacted with another department, etc.), what was done well and what could have been done better. Coaching includes the feedback component plus **providing support** and **a mutually agreed upon action plan** for enhancing the skills that lead to more successful **task and career** accomplishments in the future.

To use a golf analogy, a golf lesson is a **feedback** session. The instructor analyzes the students swing:
"You're not shifting your weight."
"You need to keep that right knee at the same angle all the way through the swing."
"Nice job of rotating your shoulders."

A coach might provide the above feedback and add:
"What is your pre-swing thought process?"
"Where do you want your game to be one year from today?"
"Let's set up a schedule for us to talk and monitor your progress."

The coach might play a round of golf with the student, providing support, inspiration and reminding the student of key techniques. The student would probably have the coach's cell phone number, in case it was needed to ask questions between formal lessons. Coaches are more than teachers, they are **partners**.

Part of being a coach is to identify coaching opportunities. These should not be limited to when you catch an SE making mistakes—that's feedback. Managers with natural coaching skills proactively seek and create opportunities. Some situations that lend themselves to coaching include when an SE:

- Clearly is struggling with a task that is within the SE's scope of responsibility
- Appears frustrated or confused
- Has displayed problems in understanding directions
- Mentions, even casually, doubts regarding ability to accomplish an important task
- Expresses a desire to develop professionally
- Comes to you directly and asks for advice, help, or coaching

Coaching is not effective when:
- Mutual respect and trust are lacking
- The coach or SE are in an elevated emotional state
- The SE is too busy or preoccupied with other tasks to pay full attention to the coaching
- The SE is disgruntled or experiencing deep job dissatisfaction
- The SE does not feel capable of meeting required expectations and is actively seeking new career options

ESSENTIAL COACHING STEPS

Coaching is a hot topic today and there are many effective coaching models to choose from. Your company may require one, specific approach or you can easily find options on-line or at your local bookstore. Whatever model you choose, it should contain the steps detailed next in order to ensure a truly comprehensive coaching experience.

The steps are culturally-mobile but need to be presented in alignment with local norms. In some parts of

Asia and Eastern Europe, for example, many have grown up with parents, teachers and governments who have told them exactly how to think and act. In these environments a very facilitative approach often doesn't work as well as the coach giving directions and taking a stronger lead position in the relationship.

A colleague of mine related an experience that reinforces this point. He was working with a senior leader of a computer chip manufacturer in Singapore. He told me that the executive had two coaches over the past few years. One coach was very facilitative and the other mostly just offered advice. He told my colleague that he was much more comfortable with the one who gave advice. This high level executive stated, *"I like to be told what to do."* This clearly would not be the case in many other cultures.

All models should contain the following steps:
1. **Set the climate**
2. **Confirm understanding of the situation**
3. **Be specific**
4. **Co-create an action plan**
5. **Summarize with benefits**
6. **Commit to next coaching session**

1. Set the climate

Carefully consider how you would like to begin the session. The initial climate you create will set the tone for the session and, if required, may be difficult to reverse. The most important factor in setting the climate for a successful coaching session is the context of the session or the session's main goals. Some climate options include:

Serious/urgent

Sometimes there will be a compelling reason for the climate to be serious and urgent. Perhaps there is a critical presentation soon after the session with a lot riding on the SE's performance. In this case you would want the SE to understand the urgency and importance of the session.

Another reason for setting a serious climate is if troublesome performance issues arise during the coaching cycle. Coaching should be supportive but SEs should leave sessions with full knowledge of their status. They should know how the coach is feeling about their progress and be aware if unacceptable issues or behaviors have emerged.

Setting a serious/urgent tone may also become important later if disciplinary actions need to be taken. Being a totally supportive and positive coach one day, and then putting an SE on a corrective plan (or worse) the next is unfair to the employee and could lead to other problems for the company.

Light/humorous

This option is appropriate when the SE is performing well and is positive about the coaching relationship. When a highly experienced SE is resistant to the coaching process, a lighter approach may seduce them into cooperation. The possible downside here is that the SE does not take the session seriously and delivering formative feedback later becomes uncomfortable or difficult. You may be the coach one day but you still need to be the manager the next.

Supportive/nurturing

Being supportive and nurturing is considered to be at the heart of coaching. Because of this, the supportive/nurturing climate might be considered a default or standard place to start. It is the safest climate and people naturally react favorably to a nurturing environment. It is also easiest to shift from this climate to a different one if required.

This approach works very well when the SE is nervous or feeling inadequate about performance. It is also fitting when the coach believes that the SE is capable and interested in performance improvement. Begin with support signals that enhance the SE's levels of comfort and security.

Empathy can play an important part in setting a supportive climate. Sharing your knowledge and experience around the challenges that face the SE will help reduce the SE's anxiety level. If possible, share a personal success story of how you were able to improve your skills or overcome barriers in the very areas in which the SE is struggling.

2. Confirm understanding of the situation

It's easy (and a common mistake) to believe that you fully understand the SE's situation based only on your observations. This is akin to an SE hearing about a customer's technical challenges and diving into prematurely recommending solutions (*"Sorry to interrupt, but I've heard this one a thousand times before. You should..."*). Instead, a skilled coach will ask probing questions that reveal more details and confirm or correct his or her initial assessment of the situation.

By investing the time to confirm your understanding, you will reinforce the coaching strategy you have planned. You will be a much more confident coach during the session if you confirm that your plan is still in alignment with the SE's needs. By taking this step you also will frequently hear new, updated data, giving you the opportunity to adjust your approach as required. This will help you avoid a situation where half way through the session an SE feels like you don't really understand his or her needs. When this happens, the SE usually will simply listen to you and feign acceptance of your guidance rather than correcting you at the risk of sounding disrespectful.

Here are two examples of questions that will help you confirm your understanding of the situation:

- *"You shared with me earlier that you'd like to be more consultative with clients. So that I can help you achieve your goal, can you tell me a little more about what exactly you mean by that?"*

- *"Your new assignment, working more closely with the Professional Services team, seems to be working out really well. You mentioned in our last meeting that you wanted them to place more value on your contributions. Ideally, what would that look like for you?"*

3. Be specific

Being specific during a coaching session increases attention and retention. Generalities like, "you present really well" or "working on your group communication skills would really help" have negligible impact. These non-specific coaching notes may actually have a negative effect, leaving the SE with doubts. The SE will wonder why he or she received such input and may later speculate incorrectly, "He said I needed to communicate clearer with groups—is it my accent?", or come to other inaccurate or potentially de-motivating conclusions.

Being specific with your coaching requires documentation. If you are going to be observing SEs as part of your coaching process, reading notes from your observations has far more impact than just appearing to pull thoughts out of the air during the session. If quoting SEs, in order to provide them with specific, real examples, it is important to capture their exact words when they are spoken. SEs will be more open to accepting the accuracy of their quotes based on documentation. An additional benefit of taking accurate notes is that SEs will appreciate the interest and effort you showed by actually writing down your observations.

In this example, a manager is going to provide coaching notes to an SE regarding the way the SE interacts with higher level managers. The manager has already set the proper climate and confirmed an understanding of the situation. Note the specificity of the feedback and the supportive tone:

****

"Tony, you've shared with me your desire to be more impactful with higher levels. One observation I have is that you change behaviors dramatically when a higher level person walks into the room. Let me give you an example. Last week at Unitech Bank, you had great, comfortable rapport with the technical team. You're really excellent at relaxing an audience. However, after Stacy, the CIO, showed up, you didn't smile once the rest of the time, even though she seemed very friendly.

You also said that you wanted to increase audience involvement. I think you are steadily improving in this area. Thursday at Unitech you were asking the group great questions like, (reading from notes) "At this point I'd like to hear from you all. What challenges or concerns do you have about migrating over to our solution?" The energy level went up and you got some great feedback.

Let's spend the next few minutes chatting about your reactions to higher levels. I have you presenting at these levels because I know you've got what it takes to impress them and succeed. So, what do you think? Any ideas as to what causes these reactions?"

✳✳

4. Co-create an action plan

As a coach you should always have clear expectations in mind before a session begins. You should have a general game plan and know your goals for the meeting.

However, this doesn't mean that you should come to a coaching session with a plan set in cement. The only way to have an SE fully embrace an action plan is to give them equal power in creating it. Once you have discussed areas that merit future action, simply ask the SE, "What do you think would help you most at this point?" If you hand an SE an action plan, it is your plan. If you co-create it, the plan becomes a partnership agreement.

Be wary of SEs who rely on you to come up with all the ideas. If they say nothing, or default to, "I don't know. What do you think, boss?", tell them to sleep on it and plan on coming in the next day with ideas. It might seem easier to just give your input and direction but then the co-creation process is lost. You are now acting as a manager, not as a coach. This approach also changes expectations for upcoming sessions. SEs who have been told to "sleep on it" before will not want to repeat this conversation and are far more likely to join you in the creativity process during future sessions.

A coaching action plan should include the following components:
- Goal(s)
- Behavioral change expectations
- Application opportunities
- Feedback process

Here is an example of a standard Action Plan:

SE:_____ COACH:_____ Date:_____	**ACTION PLAN**
Goal	Increase comfort level and effectiveness when presenting to higher level managers
Behavioral Changes	Keep the meeting interactive Maintain some tone and style throughout the meeting regardless of who shows up Project confidence with verbal and non-verbal behaviors
Application Opportunity	Thursday, 9/14, at Unitech presentation. CIO is planning to attend
Feedback process	Call coach Friday, 9/15, with self-assessment

The SE, not you, should complete the action plan. This will increase the SE's sense of ownership. Notice also that the action plan is focused on one area for improvement—presenting to higher levels. We generally recommend giving only one new goal per coaching session to avoid overwhelming the SE while enabling him or her to fully focus on just that area.

5. Summarize with Benefits

Once the action plan or next steps have been co-created, it is important that the manager and SE summarize each party's expectations for each other. This will give the SE and manager one last chance to correct any miscommunications before moving forward. Written email confirmations are recommended. Be sure that the email maintains a collaborative quality ("...to summarize, here is the action item that we agreed would be the most valuable for you to try at Monday's meeting") vs. a more aggressive and leading approach ("...here is what you committed to doing"), unless culturally desirable, as alluded to earlier in this chapter.

When summarizing, include the benefits to the SE and the organization of achieving the agreed upon coaching goals. The benefits might seem obvious, but quickly recapping them is a positive and motivational addition to the summary process. This is a step where local adjustments may be important. In Japan, for example, where team success is valued more than individual achievements, the manager might focus more on the benefits to the team than the SE.

Here are sample statements that include common benefits to SEs. The coaching goals are captured in boldface:

- "By improving your **questioning skills**, you'll learn more about what's really important to customers and you'll accomplish this in less time."
- "When account managers start giving you **more autonomy**, I think you'll find yourself in more strategic meetings, which I know you really enjoy."
- "If you're able to make **more connections between their business and our technology**, you'll start to see more deals close quicker."
- "By **separating the need to know from the nice to know** when you present, your presentations will be shorter and your message more persuasive."

- "As you become more proficient at building cross-functional relationships you'll find far more resources are available to you when you need them."

6. Commit to Next Coaching Session

Remember, one way that coaching differs from giving feedback is that coaching is an ongoing process, not an event driven trouble-shoot. Get out your calendar at the end of the session and commit to the next meeting.

By immediately committing to the next session,
you are reaffirming your commitment to the individual.

Meeting dates should be chosen carefully. Agreeing to meet every other Monday or the first Tuesday of each month may give a sense of organization yet is random and fairly meaningless. Here's a coaching conversation that demonstrates the mistake of randomly scheduling a meeting. The SE and SE manager agreed to meet the first Monday of every month.

SE manager:
"Good to see you again. I hope you had a good month. In our last session we talked about your efforts to be more engaging the next time you had a manager or executive in the room. You came up with some great ideas and I've been very excited to hear about the results."

SE:
"Yeah, that was a great session last month. I took a lot of notes."

SE manager:
"So, let's hear how you've been doing?"

SE:
"Okay, I guess."

SE manager:
"What do you mean, you guess?"

SE:
"Well, as you know, I was in new product training for two weeks last month. Then I spent two more weeks setting up and conducting the needs analysis over at Unitech. I won't be presenting anything formally for another week."

This session is not only a waste of time but reveals the manager's lack of awareness regarding the SE's schedule. At the end of the last session, the manager should have asked when the next high level presentation opportunity would occur for the SE and then scheduled the coaching session as soon as possible after that presentation. The manager could then have investigated what company the SE was presenting to and what high ranking titles were attending, leveraging that information during the next coaching session. This would have displayed a genuine interest by the manager in the coaching relationship and the SE's evolution.

A SERIOUS TIME COMMITMENT

As you can tell, coaching requires a manager to devote significant time and attention to an SE. So, be careful to only initiate a coaching relationship when you are convinced that the SE is worth the time you will be required to invest.

If you are not sure about the wisdom of committing, another option is to enter into a limited, time-bound coaching relationship. By starting with a short-term commitment you can assess the value of the coaching and the impact it has on the SE. Be sure to share this up front to avoid misleading the SE regarding the scope of the relationship.

Sample voicemail:

"Hi, Steve. I received your email and would very much like to coach you on your professional development, in particular how well you communicate and project confidence in group settings. How would you feel about having a series of meetings to discuss your progress and any ways that I can help? I'm thinking that maybe we could meet after each one of your next three presentations to discuss your progress.

Call me today and we can talk about this approach and iron out all the details. Thanks, I'm thrilled that you've expressed this interest and I look forward to being a part of your development and success."

✳✳✳

In summary, coaching provides the most intense, personal and powerful option for SE development. It can be offered to SEs who are struggling to meet expectations or to top performers, seeking to go to the next level. Because of the intense time and energy commitment required, you should be selective about who you choose to coach. When executed properly, coaching will provide team members with the support, motivation and guidance needed to help them evolve from "one place to the next.

STRATEGIC THINKING

INTRODUCTION

The evolving SE understands the need to "open the aperture," or see beyond the obvious, tactical objectives and consider the broader issues driving decision making. This section includes the most critical considerations that the evolving SE needs to analyze and address at various points during the sales cycle to be considered a strategic asset by clients and colleagues.

Chapters in this section cover the following strategic topics. You will learn how to:

- Interact in ways that shape a strategic perception
- Map client organizations by spheres of influence
- Position against competitors
- Understand and adjust to client politics
- Keep account managers happy

****

The word strategic is tossed around quite a bit in business today, with a wide variety of descriptions. One excellent description was offered by Rebecca J. Morris,

Ph.D., Associate Professor of Management at the University of Nebraska at Omaha and can be found on the University of Nebraska's website, dated 10/10/03:

"To think strategically is to be able to critically and creatively examine the complex, multi-disciplinary problems and issues that will impact organizations. Successful strategic thinking requires the ability to determine which factors are relevant to the situation and how the factors add up using a holistic perspective."

Three words in her opening sentence merit special attention as they relate to the SE world; *critically, creatively,* and *complex.* The evolving SE understands that by *critically* approaching an event and questioning traditional assumptions, new contexts and ways of looking at a situation emerge. This mindset opens the door for the possibility of *creative* solutions. We can only engage in creativity by seeing beyond the given. In addition, no matter how simple a technical assignment appears to be, there are almost always underlying *complexities,* unforeseen issues, agendas and opportunities. In spite of the amount, or lack, of information provided to SEs by clients and account managers, it is the SEs' responsibility to pursue a full understanding of these complexities.

Dr. Morris' reference to a *holistic perspective* is also on target. This ability to see the big picture by adding up all the contributing factors is another skill set that evolving SEs need to apply. Without this mindset, the technical issues at hand may become an SE's only focus, resulting in lost opportunities for initial sales and increased account penetration.

Let's say, for example, that Carrie, a software SE, is called in because a client's software program is taking too long to obtain information from another one of the client's programs. If after the first meeting Carrie comes up with a quick technical solution, she may feel as if she has done her job. She can move on to the next sales opportunity feeling successful in her performance. The client's problem is solved, a sale (albeit a small one) was made and everyone is happy.

The problem is that Carrie may have missed the opportunity to expand her company's footprint and reposition how she is perceived by the client. Yes, Carrie should have shared the solution for the immediate problem, but what if Carrie also uncovered that the reason for requesting this upgrade was to increase the speed and amount of information available to the field sales team? Maybe Carrie's company would have had other products and services that would address this issue beyond the quick fix.

This higher level focus could increase the potential size of the deal (see chapter 9 of this section, *"Keeping Account Managers Happy"*) and maybe open the door for a better, more strategic solution. This need for, as Dr. Morris says, a *"holistic"* perspective, is one of many compelling reasons for you to read and apply the information in the chapters that follow on the evolving SE as a strategic thinker.

Chapter 5

BEING PERCEIVED AS STRATEGIC

Instead of fighting over the slice, make the pie bigger.

Atypical client conversation might sound like this:

Client (CIO):

"We need to integrate the different applications we now run, so we're looking for someone who can make that happen quickly and cost effectively. Tom, your account manager, said that you would be in charge of the technical analysis."

SE (Juanita):

"Yes, I'll be the leader of our technical team. Based on what Tom has told me, I thought I'd start by giving you an overview of our latest solution, FireApp. It's really interesting. Our software is able to integrate applications by using a new technology that provides a customizable dashboard. Here's an example slide now."

How does this sound? Juanita is polite, passionate about her product and prepared to give a full explanation of its features and benefits. So far, so good? Actually, so far, so boring and off-target! Juanita is falling into the trap of diving into the technology (probably her comfort zone) and ignoring the bigger picture. Plus, this is the CIO. When Juanita begins in this manner, what is the CIO's impression of her? How is she being categorized (which people naturally do) in terms of her contribution to the sales process? The answer is that she has pigeon-holed herself as a technical expert who is more interested in talking than listening.

Being known as the most knowledgeable technical resource on the team is, of course, a positive. In fact, it's the price of admission for being an SE. However, if SEs are going to evolve to a position where they are asked to assist in defining and creating the larger, strategic vision, more is required.

When SEs are perceived as strategic assets there are many benefits, particularly as they relate to upper levels. When this perception is evoked, managers and executives:

- **Become more available in the future**
- **Invite the SE to join road mapping meetings**
- **Believe that they will learn something valuable from the SE**
- **Consider the SE's value a differentiating factor in the final buying decision**

1. Become more available in the future

Why spend time with a purely technical SE when upper levels already have numerous reports charged with evaluating technology and providing them with technical summaries? Levels such as CIO, VP, or line of business executive usually will not interact much with an SE outside of the initial meeting and when attending presentations.

If, for example, the CIO meets with an SE early in the process, this early involvement is usually to synthesize the organization's needs and ensure goal clarity. The CIO is the business executive charged with mapping IT initiatives to the goals of the organization and will likely only interact within this context.

In our example above, Juanita was able to interact with the CIO early in the sales cycle. If approached as modeled above, the CIO is likely to end the meeting by identifying who Juanita should contact from now on. The message is likely to be, *"Work with Steve from now on,"* and *"See you at the final presentation."*

If Juanita is perceived as more of a value-add, strategic thinker, the reaction and relationship might be different. The CIO might, for example, take calls from her or agree to occasional email communications. Having consistent communication with key stakeholders as high up the ladder as possible should be one of Juanita's goals in the account. This will keep her abreast of shifting managerial considerations. It will also result in others within the organization recognizing the upper level respect that she is receiving. When others note this respect, they are more likely to treat her with elevated respect as well.

2. Invite the SE to join future, strategic meetings

One misconception in sales is that clients are reticent to invite vendor SEs to internal strategic meetings.

When SEs hear that such meetings will take place, too often the reaction is polite and defensive, such as, *"Great, I'll look forward to the results of your meeting."* When SEs have built a desired, strategic image, they are very likely to be invited to these sessions and should even be comfortable **asking permission** to attend.

SEs earn a place at the table during strategic meetings when they are perceived as:
- Mature
- Possessing more knowledge on the topic than the customer's technical team
- Relating their technology to the big picture
- Trustworthy with confidential information
- Adding value through comments **and** questions
- Sensitive to only participating or interjecting when they truly have something of value to add
- Concise and focused when they do comment

When SEs meet this criteria they are no longer perceived as "the vendor" but have elevated their status in significant ways. However, even if you possess all of the above traits, you may still have to wait a good amount of time until full trust is established. Clients still need some time to observe your style and how you handle yourself in group settings. Pushing for early involvement in strategic sessions before building the desired reputation may make the client defensive and delay your involvement even further. Instead, be patient, model the traits above and you will be pleased at how quickly you are invited to these meetings.

Of course, you should understand that there are some topics that naturally exclude vendor SEs from attendance. These include when clients are discussing:
- Your competition
- Budget
- Negotiation strategies
- Employee performance issues
- "Turf wars" or internal conflicts that might reveal weaknesses that a vendor could leverage

You should not aggressively pursue meetings where these topics are on the agenda. Your involvement may raise concerns regarding your lack of boundaries and even ethics. Hopefully, you can identify an internal champion who is willing to share some of the data points that emerge from these discussions.

3. Believe that they will learn something valuable from the SE

Upper levels are anxious and open to investing time with an objective third party from whom they believe they will learn something of significant, tangible value. They want to be motivated to analyze critical areas in a different light based on the inspirational qualities of the conversation. Managers value and seek those whose outside view can help them see pitfalls and opportunities that they cannot.

One popular way to impact this area is to position yourself as the roving eyes and ears for managers and executives. Many at higher levels don't want to, or don't have the time to, wander around or personally engage personnel, even though these individuals may have valuable "shop floor" insights.

You, as the evolving SE, with access to so many, have a grand opportunity to synthesize and communicate team data back up the ladder.

For example, here is a discussion between a manager or executive (Sarah) and you, the SE, interested in elevating the relationship:

"Sarah, thanks for meeting with me today. I've been speaking with a wide cross section of your team, from architects to named account consultants. What I've discovered is that there are some common mindsets in the field that I thought you'd find interesting.

In particular, most people I've spoken with see free shareware as the number one threat facing your business today. In fact, customers are starting to talk about this price-to-value topic more frequently. My sense is that it would be helpful for your people to be armed with a consistent response to offer when clients raise this issue."

Three very good things may happen as a result of this interaction. Sarah may:

1. Take away new and important information to share with other managers and above
2. Have her "gut feeling" about this issue reinforced
3. Reframe how she perceives you. You have now positioned yourself as her eyes and ears in the field, and she may very well come back to you later, seeking other valuable input.

4. Consider the SE's value a differentiating factor in the decision process

Almost all organizations will have well-defined decision criterion for significant investments. The criterion items are usually weighted.

Traditional criteria include:
    a.   **Technical performance**
    b.   **Price**
    c.   **Delivery**
    d.   **Training**
    e.   **International support capabilities**
    f.   **References**
    g.   **Experience of sales/implementation team**
    h.   **Flexibility**

Not listed here are less tangible items that carry notable weight and almost certainly impact decision making. If, for example, a client's technical team tells management about positive experiences that they are having with one pre-sales team over the other (responsiveness professionalism, etc.) this could affect the final decision.

Often a pre-sales experience is negative. Maybe the vendor does not respond in a timely manner or they are perceived as arrogant and over-confident. When this occurs, decision teams will often lower the weight of harder, stated criterion items to avoid unpleasant partnerships. The proof of this theory is in how many deals go to vendors with acceptable, yet inferior technology. When this occurs, the certain front runner is left wondering, *"How did we possibly lose that deal?"*

There are many ways for SEs to make their personal value a bigger part of the final decision. For example, let's say that you are competing against an evenly matched competitor. One major difference is that they offer inexpensive on-line training. Your company requires costly classroom training for users. Money is one part of the equation but the main benefit to the client is how much time they will save with self-paced, on-line training.

Your account manager is resigned to the fact that this deficiency could cost your company the deal. He or she has tried diligently to uncover an advantage on other criteria items to counter this training issue, but to no avail.

Early in the process (thanks to the mapping skills that you will learn about later) you identified Ron, a Lead Technical Manager, as a huge influencer. Ron has been with the company for over 10 years and was personally recruited by the CEO.

You have gone out of your way to build your relationship with Ron, including finding a white paper on a topic that he had expressed an interest in exploring. He was thrilled with your proactive gesture. This white paper contained strategic ideas very aligned with some of the goals mentioned by the CEO at this year's sales kick-off. You shared with Ron that you are aware of other resources on the topic and also keep a record of client interests. If Ron has other topics he would like information on, you would be glad to search your database and keep him posted of future discoveries that you think he might be interested in seeing.

You have also gleaned through your questioning and observing skills that Ron has his eye on a VP position that just opened up. Presenting the white paper and similar ideas to his superiors would certainly help him appear more strategic and high-level in his approach—just the kind of thinking that they are looking for in a VP.

Can this kind of activity really impact from whom a client chooses to buy their products and services? Put yourself in Ron's position and you will soon realize that the answer is a resounding *"Yes."* The complimentary and unexpected value that evolved SEs bring to the business *and* personal needs of the client, beyond the *Request for Proposal* criterion checklist, often determines the fate of a sale.[1]

****

THE BIG PICTURE

In order to be perceived as strategic, SEs need to begin discussions at a high level and drill down from there. Based on who the SEs are interacting with, they should focus on understanding the client's defined *vision* and *higher business purpose* before technical issues are explored. A simple idiom all SEs should remember is:

Start as strategic as the client's role dictates.

Interacting with a developer may result in a strategic question that sounds pretty tactical in nature, such as, *"What would you ideally like to change about your development process?"* The answer is likely to be technical but you may hear something far more interesting that leads you down a new path, such as *"The process is fine, we just never* know what the priorities are around here." As you call higher, the client's role dictates different questions, such as "How do you want end users to perceive your website as a result of our work?"

It takes very little time for an SE to consider the other party's focus and develop more strategic questions. I know SEs are going in the right direction when they directly say to a client, "Let's start with the big picture."

****

Contrast this conversation with the one at the beginning of this chapter:

Client (CIO):
"We need to integrate the different applications we now run, so we're looking for someone who can make that happen quickly and cost effectively. Tom, your account manager, said that you would be in charge of the technical analysis."

SE (Juanita):
"Yes, I'll be the leader of our technical team. If it's okay with you, I'd like to start with a few big picture questions to make sure that whatever I recommend is in alignment with your goals. These should take no more than ten minutes. After that I should be able to give you initial ideas regarding next steps. How does that sound?"

Client (CIO):
"I only have 20 minutes so that sounds fine. Go ahead."

SE (question examples):

"What's your main motivation or reason for exploring this change now?"

"What would an ideal system accomplish for the organization?"

"What other strategic initiatives might be impacted by our work?"

✳✳✳

Occasionally I will hear pushback on this idea from SEs such as, *"Sometimes they just want a technical explanation."* Situationally, this may be true, particularly when the other party is:

· **Highly technical** (programmer, architect, etc.)
· **In panic mode** (a process is inoperable and needs immediate fixing)
· **Getting impatient with the sales process** (other team members have already asked "big picture" questions)
· **Expecting a demonstration** (SEs should meet any predetermined expectations)

These all represent valid reasons for leading with a purely technical focus. However, what we often find is that these and other reasons are used as excuses by SEs for not attempting to start discussions at a higher level. Please remember that when you are able to probe and better understand the big picture, you are creating a win for you and the client. Your team will possibly be able to expand the scope of its proposal and the customer may be offered options that will address far more critical issues than solving the obvious, short-term technical challenge.

✳✳✳

In summary, being perceived as strategic has tremendous value for SEs and their clients. For SEs, in addition to obtaining richer information that can be leveraged during proposal design, building this image can change how decisions are made, even when stated decision criterion already exists. For clients, an outside eye that can see the forest from the trees may be able to introduce creative, breakthrough options that go far beyond the tactical, short-term needs that were the relationship's initial focus.

Evolving SEs are also strategic in how they approach a client from an *organizational* perspective. Next you will learn how to map a client's organization by spheres of influence—an activity that will lead to better time allocation for you and more focused and effective account penetration planning for the team.

More on this topic later in Chapter 19, Satisfying Personal Needs.

Chapter 6

MAPPING
CLIENT ORGANIZATIONS

There are many excellent sales training programs available that teach salespeople how to execute strategic account planning. These are usually taught in two to four-day formats, are very comprehensive and include multi-page planning forms that the salespeople are then expected to complete out in the field.

These courses are excellent for AMs but, in our experience and based on client feedback, are often overkill for SE teams. SEs who have experienced such training tell us that they learn quite a bit and enjoy the sessions. They also say that they probably will not use at least half of the ideas presented and never fill out the extensive planning forms, unless required by their managers.

In over 15 years of working with SE organizations I have yet to find an SE manager who makes this kind of detailed planning work a required activity. SE managers must be thoughtful and deliberate in deciding how SEs allocate their time. This lack of enthusiasm around enforcing the completion of elaborate planning forms or processes tells me that SE managers simply do not see the value.

At Technically Speaking we have found that SEs have a definite threshold of pain when it comes to completing planning forms. As a result, our rule of thumb is that the size of sales planning forms is limited to a maximum of **one piece of paper**. It can be double sided, but one piece only! In part because of this rule, we have been told that our planners are utilized in the field. The mapping planner in this section abides by this "one piece only" rule.

Mapping will benefit SEs in many ways, including helping them to identify:
- **How decisions are made**
- **How they should allocate their time**
- **At whom they should focus the content of proposals and presentations**
- **Where the trap doors or deal-killers lurk**
- **Current and potential internal champions**

SEs do not, and should not, have to uncover all this information on their own. AMs should provide much of this data based on their discovery work. However, with SEs' unique relationships, they may often uncover rich data during seemingly innocuous conversations. For example, an innocent comment like, "*I'm just going to run this by Steve in Development,*" may be an indicator that a new decision maker has joined the process.

To help uncover this kind of valuable information, evolving SEs work on mapping the client's organization throughout the sales cycle. As you will see, this goes well beyond constructing an organizational chart. The map you build will be an organic document, with an ongoing need for analysis and change. Particularly in longer sales cycles, client organizational changes will dictate diligent attention to making appropriate mapping changes and shifting sales strategies as needed, sometimes on a moment's notice.

Here are the categories and definitions of the annotations on the map that follows. The final category, *Threatened*, is the only one that I have provided detail on. The other category definitions should be self-evident.

Decision Influence (DI):

5 – Final veto power
4 – Makes final recommendation
3 – Evaluation committee member
2 – Product Implementer
1 – Negligible involvement in decision process

Support Network (SN):

++ – Strong supporter
+ – Supporter
? – Undecided, neutral
X – Adversary
CX – Adversary and champion of a competitive offering

Threatened (TH):

Threatened   Not Threatened

New technology has always produced a variety of employee reactions. Going back to the Industrial Revolution, mass production was embraced by management as the ultimate profit opportunity. Employees had different opinions on this direction and not always negative. Many saw mass production as a means to ensure company longevity, profitability and job security. Many of these workers were immigrants, coming from areas that offered precious few options. ANY work was appreciated, particularly if no previous training or language capabilities were required. This was the position of my ancestors.

To others these new machines were instruments of torture. In order to make a living, one had to engage in back-breaking work, in unhealthy conditions, for years on end. Children as young as four were employed in production factories with dangerous, and often fatal, working conditions. Workers of every age would routinely work up to 16 hours per day.

While many *physical* hardships in the workplace continue today, particularly in under developed regions, technology has created hardships that are more *emotional* in nature. The following is a fictitious story with a fictitious character. But read the story and see if it doesn't sound familiar to you.

****

THE NEW WAY

Jon has been with United Freight Alliance (UFA) for most of his 15 year career. UFA is a well know and profitable international shipping company. Jon graduated with a Computer Science degree and joined UFA after a brief stint with Microsoft. From day one, Jon has been a star with UFA, mainly because of the value he has brought to the IT department.

Jon's specialty is his ability to integrate disparate software applications. For example, Sales recently requested an easier way to access customer records. Currently, the sales software program only gives pricing and delivery information. They have requested that information on the customer's accounting records be available on their system as well. Knowing how much a customer has purchased and where they stand in terms of payment status would be great to know out in the field.

The problem is that the sales and accounting systems are from different vendors. UFA has no plans to scrap these systems (individually they work great) but sees the value in this request.

This request is right in Jon's power wheel. He is great at writing programs that will integrate these kinds of applications. He has told Sales and management that this should take about two months and then everything will be fine. As he is not all that busy right now he is thrilled to have the assignment. In fact, with profits down again this quarter, there are rumors that cuts might have to be made and that no one is safe. Not that he feels threatened, but Jon has some big bills coming up (two kids going to college soon and a new roof) and would hate to have to deal with an unexpected financial crisis.

One good thing going for Jon is that no one else in the company can do what he does. In fact, in confidence, Jon tells his friends that he has intentionally not taught others in the company what he knows. Or, as Jon puts it, *"Hey, if they know everything that I know, what happens to my value?"*

Jon's boss, Terry, calls Jon into her office later that week. They have the following conversation:

Terry:

"Hi Jon, thanks for coming in. How's it going?"

Jon:

"Excellent, Terry. I'm really excited about helping sales with this latest software request. As you saw in my report, I don't expect this to take longer than two months."

Terry:

"That's what I wanted to talk to you about. We know you can do it but we've been looking at other options."

Jon:
(Getting a sinking feeling in his stomach)
"Other options? You mean like giving the work to someone else?"

Terry:

"Not within UFA. We've actually had some great discussions with a company called Linkage. Have you heard of them?"

Jon:

"Yeah, I've heard of them. Aren't they pretty expensive?

Terry:

"*That remains to be seen. Steve (Director of IT) has asked me to cooperate with Linkage so that they can conduct a needs analysis and come back to us with a proposal. I'd like you to meet with their SE and help him out in whatever ways you can.*"

Jon:

"*Yeah, of course. When will he be here?*"

Terry:

"*He's actually here today and I've got you slotted to meet with him in 45 minutes. I know that this may be a little challenging for you, seeing as you've been our only option up until now, but we do need you to cooperate fully.*"

Jon:

"*Of course. Can I just ask, are you looking at Linkage for this job only or for other similar needs?*"

Terry:

"*We really don't know yet but obviously anything that can save us time and money is worth considering. In fact (laughing) they said that they could complete this sales request in just two weeks! Imagine that...*"

Jon:
(Forcing a smile)
"*Yeah, imagine that...*"

****

Does this sound realistic? Possible? How about likely? This type of story is commonplace in corporations today. "Security" in just about every role, particularly fast-changing departments like IT, has a much looser definition. Hording information and hiding in your cubicle waiting for retirement is no longer a career option.

One important note about this conversation between Jon and Terry is that the **SE from Linkage was not present**. When the *Linkage* SE sits down with Jon to conduct the needs analysis, he will have no idea about what just transpired. No one has handed him a dossier detailing Jon's career path, his choice to horde information and his upcoming financial obligations.

Picture what the initial meeting between Jon and the SE will look like? My guess is that Jon will be cooperative, but minimally. He will filter his answers to the SE's questions, being careful not to share any additional data that could further erode his power. He will not volunteer additional, valuable insights but will instead limit the scope of his answers. He will not proactively help the SE gain access to important resources that the SE might find to be extremely helpful. Jon will be professional, aloof and guarded.

Imagine how Jon would react if the SE goes into a sales pitch about the value of his solutions? This could possibly happen if the SE senses Jon's lack of enthusiasm and decides to "sell" him on the great products and services that Linkage represents. The more the SE pumps up Linkage, the more Jon will feel threatened and upset. This misread by the SE would dramatically increase the negative reaction and resentment Jon already feels towards the SE and Linkage.

Almost any significant change leads to someone feeling threatened.

Because of this present-day reality, we have included a "Threatened" box in the planner. Simply place an "X" in the "TH" box if you sense that the person feels threatened by your technology, as Jon experienced in our story. This threat-reaction may manifest itself in the form of revealing comments, or hostility or disinterest towards you with no rational justification.

Decision Influence (DI):
5 – Final veto power
4 – Makes final recommendation
3 – Evaluation committee member
2 – Product Implementer
1 – Negligible involvement in decision process

Support Network (SN):
++　　– Strong supporter
+　　　– Supporter
?　　　– Undecided, neutral
X　　　– Adversary
CX　　– Adversary and champion of a
competitive offering

Threatened (TH):

CLIENT MAP

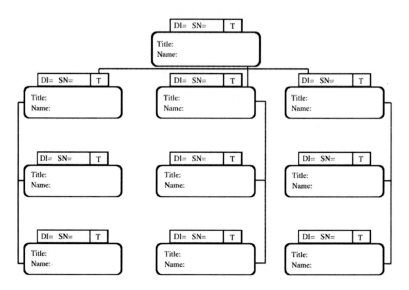

Below is an example of client mapping. Review the map and think about what you would recommend for next steps if this was your account:

CLIENT MAP

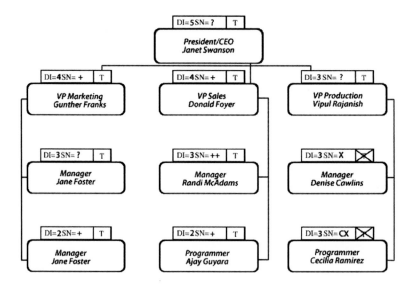

What lessons can be learned from this mapping?

- Starting at the top, Janet, the President/CEO, has no bias at this point (that we are aware of) and would prefer that others come to her with final recommendations. The team needs to work harder to uncover her needs and any other hidden agendas as she does hold final veto power.

- We seem to have pretty good support on the sales and marketing side. Perhaps the benefits of our proposal are more slanted to their needs.

- Randi McAdams is our best candidate to be an internal champion.

- Even from the purely technical side, we are favored in Sales and Marketing by both programmers. They are apparently holding the perception that our products/services will help them be more productive, create a higher quality product or make their jobs easier. It would be interesting to know which. They do not perceive us as a threat.

- Reservations and doubts exist in Production. Even down to the programmer level, we have detractors. Have we not met their needs? Do they not feel like they have been included in the process? Why do Denise and Cecilia feel threatened? How would they define a "win" for themselves in this purchase?

· One answer to Production's management concerns could be that Cecilia is a "CX." This bias may be floating up to her manager (who is an "X" but not a "CX") or going the other way, with the manager affecting the programmer's feelings. More focused questions are needed to uncover the real objections and concerns.

· Some good news is that the VP of Production is a "3" vs. a "4" on the influence scale. This can be due to many reasons. Maybe this product does not impact him as much as Sales and Marketing or maybe he is relatively new with the company and lacks influence. So while we need to address concerns in Production, it is important not to dilute the power of the message that Sales and Marketing (who have more power) have embraced.

****

You may be wondering when to construct this kind of client map. After all, particularly early in the relationship, you will probably not know many of the names and variables required to complete the map properly.

As alluded to previously, this map will be a living document. It will be updated throughout the sales cycle. Three recommended opportunities for working with the map are:

· **At the beginning of the sales cycle**
Usually your AMs will have had some initial contacts before involving you in the sale. Ask your account man-

agers if they can provide you with the information they have learned to help you get your map started. In addition to providing you with valuable data, this also sends the message to your AMs that the map will be an ongoing tool and contributor to the sales process and they should expect to have their input solicited on a regular basis.

· **Immediately following client meetings**

When you finish a client meeting, go to your template and make appropriate updates and additions. Be sure to share your findings with AMs and other team members.

· **Before crafting/presenting proposals**

Information from the map should be examined when crafting and presenting proposals. Questions like, *"How do we prioritize our product's benefits in the proposal?"* can often be answered by simply reviewing your map.

✳✳

In summary, part of being a strategic SE is your ability to accurately assess the influence and decision-making landscape of a client's organization. In this chapter you learned how to map client spheres of influence in an extremely time-efficient manner. By working with your AM to fully understand these roles and influences you will be in the best position to decide on your priorities and next steps. In the next chapter, you will further enhance your value by learning how to powerfully position your company against the competition.

Chapter 7

REACTING TO COMPETITION

Let's say that you are an SE, working closely with a customer to define their technical needs. You are alone in a meeting with the Lead Technical Manager and Director of IT (the account manager is outside making a call) when the Director of IT says:

"We're not sure which way to go at this point. We are talking to another provider who seems to be a little stronger in terms of offering a more flexible package."

Wait until you tell the account manager what you just heard!

In addition, would you:
· Ask who the competitor is?
· Probe for a better understanding of what the competition offers?
· Tell the client why you are better than your competitors?
· Avoid asking the client anything else about the competition and just tell your account manager about the comment?

Like most answers to sales-related questions, the answer is, *"It depends."* Many AMs want to handle competitive discussions personally. This can be based on personal preferences or situational elements. For example, let's say that your AM, Martha, is well versed in the competitor's offerings. In this case she may be very excited about conducting an apples-to-apples comparison. Maybe Martha has successfully conducted comparisons against this particular competitor before or even worked for them at some point and dreams of an opportunity like this. If she finds out that you decided to take the initiative and begin the comparison, she might react angrily, believing that, no matter how well you did, she could have done better. In this case, she would understandably want to do the "selling" on her own. So, one rule for SEs to remember when the competition is mentioned is:

Know your boundaries.

Know your boundaries as defined by the AM, your manager and other key players on the team. If you are not sure, ask. Quote the example above and ask what reaction they would recommend. This will give them the increased comfort and trust to allow you to function autonomously, while protecting you against any back-lashes from taking well-intended, yet ill-advised approaches.

That said, as an evolving SE you should be *capable* of positioning against the competition and reacting effectively in such a situation. Maybe your AM is not well-versed against a particular competitor. Maybe your depth of technical knowledge makes you a more credible candidate to discuss the differences with them. Maybe your

AM expects SEs to react proactively in these situations. Whatever the reasons, the evolving SE needs to be ready when the client mentions the competition.

When done properly, exploring the competitive landscape is likely to:
· Provide valuable data for the rest of your team
· Yield information that changes how your team's proposals and presentations are executed
· Reposition how you are perceived by your team (yes, you can be looked on as a "trusted advisor" within your own company)

Remember, because the client does not view you as a pure salesperson, you have unique credibility and cache that should be leveraged. Obviously you are there to help make a sale but when SEs inquire about competitive products it is commonly viewed as technical inquisitiveness and curiosity. When AMs probe about the competition it tends to come off like they are searching for holes in the competition's ideas or proposals. In fact, in our earlier example, the customer might not have even raised the concern about your proposal if the AM was present.

It is important to note that it is actually an **advantage to your client** for them to tell you about your competition. They are looking for the best solution and if you know about your competitor's proposal, then you are able to more accurately contrast for the client how you will address the client's needs vs. your approach.

For example, let's say that the client tells you that your competitor is including some free software that will enable the client to get some of their software packages to communicate with each other. You are very familiar with this free software. Many others have told you that what appears to be "free" actually becomes very costly over the long haul. Once you are given the software you then have to pay very high fees for training and support. The support packages in particular are extremely costly. Only experienced programmers can really support the product on their own so almost every client ends up paying exorbitant fees to keep the software running.

Would the client benefit from you sharing this knowledge? Absolutely. The point is that by sharing competitive information with competing vendors, clients are setting up a checks and balances system that leads to more complete information, resulting in better informed decisions.

It is also an advantage to your client from a *negotiation angle* to talk about the competition. Just knowing that there is competition builds in the expectation of give and take. Clients will expect you to share competitive information with your AMs. Any proposed action items or price discussions now must be approached with sensitivity to what the competition might offer. Also, as alluded to earlier, presentations are more likely to contain competitive comparison data, further educating the client.

When the client mentions competition they may bring up topics that are beyond the scope of the SE. For example, if you are asked about discounts, free support or other concessions, get out of the way!

Here are examples of statements that SEs should *avoid* making when the competition is mentioned:

Client:
> *"Your competitor is a lot cheaper for the same package."*

SE:

- ✔ *"I don't get involved in pricing but I'm sure my account manager will be as flexible as possible."*
- ✔ *"I don't get involved in pricing but you should know that we don't really discount."*
- ✔ *"I don't get involved in pricing but I know that we'll do whatever it takes to get your business."*

These may sound silly but some forms of these are actually quite common. Simply state, *"I don't get involved in pricing discussions. You'll need to speak with _____ (my AM) about that."* and then stop talking!

If your boundaries dictate a proactive involvement in exploring the competition then you should courageously broach the topic. One key to successfully understanding the competitive landscape is to:

Frame the reason for your interest in a way that benefits the client.

Have a reason to share with the client that makes it important and acceptable for your questions. Include any benefits that are material and relevant to the client as well.

Example:

Director of IT:

"We're not sure which way to go at this point. We are talking to another provider who seems to be a little stronger in terms of offering a more flexible package."

SE:

"In order to make sure that we propose a package that meets all your needs regarding flexibility, can you tell me more about what they are proposing that you're finding so appealing?"

Is it possible that they will say, *"No."* We can never predict the other party's reaction. However, this framing technique should make it seem reasonable enough to the customer for them to provide you with some data points. Why not tell you what is so great about the other offer? Maybe you will match it! Or, if the Director is speaking without hard facts to back him or her up (maybe the comment is based on second or third hand information) this will ferret out the shaky foundation on which the comment stands.

Notice also that the SE did not ask who the competition is. There is no need. Based on the information the SE receives and the team's knowledge of the market, the competitor should be obvious. If not, carefully planned questions could be asked later to verify their identity.

✴✴

When the client offers competitive information, your gut reaction is likely to tell them why you are better. Resist!

Example:

Client:

"*They have a lot of other products that we can add as options later that you don't offer. It's appealing to be able to have the same vendor just connect the new programs as we need them. If we go with you, we will have to go to new vendors for other products and that can lead to finger pointing when there's a problem.*"

SE:

"*I know that they have other products but from what I hear those products are just not state of the art, plus they're going to charge you an arm and a leg to install and support them.*"

The client may then counter with another point ("*They showed me the prices for add-on modules and they were quite cheap.*"), which you then counter ("*Yeah but you get what you pay for and you'll have to spend a lot of time and money to get those customized.*"), then they counter, and on and on. You are no longer having a discussion, you're having a debate! In addition to this scenario, there are many other reasons to avoid immediately trying to counter or "one up" the competition. They include:

- It makes you look like an amateur in terms of dealing with objections
- It makes you look defensive
- If you are number one in your market (or want to be perceived as such) you should not negatively or directly discuss the competition[1]
- You probably are countering their claim before fully understanding their position
- There may be a competitive supporter present, causing tension and animosity

- By gathering information, going away and then strategizing with your team, you will probably come up with a much more effective response than an initial, emotional reaction

Once you have had a chance to think about the competition and what the client has said, there are many options for dealing with the threat. One of the most important rules to remember is that **you want the focus to be on your advantages, not the competition's weaknesses.**

That may seem like a minor distinction but it's quite an important one. If you spend more than 15% of your time in any one meeting talking about what they have or don't have, you are going in a bad direction. Just think how you would feel listening to a vendor go on and on about the shortcomings of a competitor. Connected to this is an important statement to remember:

You are not an expert on your competition.

You may know about their product, you may be able to explain their product and you may even be able to operate their product, but you *do not know* what they internally announced this morning. You *were not* at the last training session regarding new features. You should avoid the temptation to believe or act in any ways that indicate that you consider yourself an expert on their product. Knowledgeable? Yes. An expert? No.

Competition Bashing

One account manager shared a story with me about an SE who mercilessly bashed the competition in front of the client. This SE had worked for the competitor up until about 90 days before the presentation and thought he really had the goods on them. He pointed out their lack of a specific product feature and rested his case for not buying from them on this deficiency in their product line.

The customer's team had a sadly predictable response. First, they told him that the competitor's SE had just demonstrated that new feature. It had been released 45 days ago and the demonstration was flawless. They next asked the SE why he wasn't working for them anymore. The SE, obviously flustered, went down a rat hole of embarrassing, personal reasons including his frustration that "I just didn't want to work that many Saturdays anymore." By the end of the meeting he had lost all credibility and was immediately taken off the account.

To make matters worse, word got out about his performance and, particularly because he was the new kid on the block, other AMs resisted using him. After just over a year of his uphill battle to erase first impressions, he left the company.

If you properly frame your reason for gathering competitive data and are able to probe further, you have three options for what to do with the competitive information.

Choices include:
- **Conduct an apples-to-apples comparison**
- **Change the playing field**
- **Plant landmines**

CONDUCT AN APPLES-TO-APPLES COMPARISON

As alluded to earlier, this is dangerous because you are spending so much time discussing the competition. This approach is advisable if you are quite certain that, given this direct comparison, the client will find you favorable. This would be true if there are specific product or company features that can be verified and you *know* give you a distinct advantage. One of the best verification sources would be an internal champion who has recently seen a competitive presentation or proposal and is certain about product deficiencies.

It is also the best way to ensure that similar packages are being proposed. On the surface, many proposals appear almost identical but after an apples-to-apples comparison, material differences can surface.

Example:

Client:

"We just don't see a whole lot of difference between you two but you're 10% more expensive."

SE:

"Let's make sure that you really are getting the same value from each of us. The best way to do that is to conduct a real apples-to-apples comparison of the proposal. Is that okay with you?"

Clients are likely to cooperate, particularly if the deal is complex and contains numerous line items and negotiables. If a client does not want to conduct the comparison, simply ask them why. If they feel it would be too time consuming or not worth the effort then the reality may be that they were never seriously considering your solution in the first place. Maybe the technical buyer was told to get at least three bids and you are number three. So, requesting the apples-to-apples comparison can act as a qualifier as well. If you are truly in the running, the client should be open to this process.

CHANGE THE PLAYING FIELD

This can be a very effective way to elevate your team above the competition. It can be accomplished if you are certain of a critical area where you clearly prevail. Refocus the conversation to this area, bolstering its value to the overall decision.

In any sales arena, it is best to get the customer to "sell themselves" vs. you trying to convince them. A sales adage that support this says,

If I say it, you can doubt me. If you say it, it's true.

Let's say, for example, that you would like to change the playing field to the topic of global support capabilities. You feel like you have a clear advantage in this area and would benefit by placing more attention on this point. Begin by asking one or two questions designed to have the client reinforce the importance of global support:

1. *"How important is it to have immediate support with on-site capabilities in some of your satellite offices like Mumbai or Helsinki?"*
2. *"What would happen if the support is late or ineffective?"*

If you have done your homework correctly you should receive a predictable, positive response. If you have missed something along the way or the criterion has shifted, i.e. they don't heavily value global support, you would want to confirm this before changing the playing field to an area of relatively lower weight.

Next, deliver a statement that focuses attention on this area of strength for your company.

Example:
"In all of our discussions with you and your team we've heard about the importance of global support capabilities to the success of this initiative and some of the consequences of not performing exceptionally well in this area. While many offer these capabilities to some extent, we believe we have the deepest resources available in every one of the international cities where you have a presence. Because of the importance of support to your global success, we feel that this is a difference truly worth considering as you make your final decision."

This can come off as self-serving and heavy-handed if not done properly. This is particularly true if you choose to change the playing field to an area of relatively low importance. Subtly, assertively, change the playing field only after confirming its value. Do not directly degrade or discuss the competition.

PLANT LANDMINES

How many serious competitors do you have? Three? Five? Because most companies that are not in a commodity business have such a finite set of competitors, there really is no excuse for not knowing their weaknesses. This information is usually available from AMs, other customers and Marketing.

Knowing their weaknesses allows you to plant the questions in your clients' minds that you want them to ask your competition. Think for a moment about your company's greatest weakness. What question should the competition be planting in your clients' minds to ask you?

Have you ever had a question from a customer that really threw you off? It was so on-target in exposing a major weakness that it made you wonder how they knew to ask about such a deficient area. They may have gotten that question from your competition. Assume that your competitors are using this technique. This is a very acceptable sales tactic that you should be comfortable employing.

Example:

"As you do your due diligence and comparisons we feel that there are three questions that are important to ask all contenders. They are:

1. *What are your capabilities for training a large number of users quickly?*
2. *How would you handle a support issue for our Munich office if it requires an on-site visit?*

3. *What references do you have in the insurance industry implementing this exact application?"*

The reality is that your customers will know what you are doing. They are well aware that you are favorably comparing yourself against the competition without mentioning them. However, if this is done professionally and the bullet items are important, their reaction should be accepting and even appreciative. In fact, you are saving them time by providing questions that will expose potential deficiencies and allow competitors the chance to respond. Finally, don't expect your customers to remember these questions. Put them in a handout, in your proposal, in a follow up email or somewhere they can easily find them.

✳✳

In summary, as an SE you are working in a highly competitive world where almost every new opportunity requires you and your team to outperform and outsell the competition. Meet with your team to know your boundaries regarding dealing with the competition and know how aggressive you can be when opportunities to respond surface. When flexibility is granted, your ability to uncover competitive data and related customer perceptions will add tremendous value to the sales effort, while significantly enhancing your image and reputation with team members as well.

(1) A classic advertising adage is that #1 in the market does not mention #2. A case in point can be seen with the #1 soft drink company, Coca-Cola. You will notice that they never mention Pepsi, but in 2011 Pepsi ran an ad

campaign showing the Coca-Cola Santa Claus on vacation in Mexico drinking Pepsi! An interesting aside is that up until the mid 1970s, it was illegal in the United States to make disparaging remarks about a competitor's product in an advertisement.

Chapter 8

UNDERSTANDING OFFICE POLITICS

"Politics is more difficult than physics."
Albert Einstein

"Being 'best of breed' is useless if you don't know how decisions are really made."
SE Manager

Have you ever lost a deal even though you clearly had the best technology or solution? When the decision was announced, some innocuous reason was given to your team like, *"We just felt that overall they offered a better package."* One possible reason for this event, as mentioned in Chapter 5, is that the competitor's SEs were able to make their personal contributions a larger part of the decision criterion. Another possibility is the unforeseen impact of office politics.

Office politics is endemic to organizations. While management may try to position its workforce as united, with one, common goal, people come to work with many

145

goals, including personal ones that may conflict with organizational aspirations. These goals lead to conflict and competition amongst employees for the allocation of scarce resources, including time. This competition manifests itself in many unproductive ways, including the surfacing of office politics. According to a July, 2002 survey of 1,500 managers by SCQuaRE Management Consultants, UK, office politics is estimated to cost the UK British economy £6.2 billion a year in lost productivity.

Office politics can make it seem as if decisions are based on mysterious criteria that you are not privy to knowing. Office politics make people behave in irrational ways and make inexplicable decisions. They may be overt and obvious or subtle and surprising. They may surface in the form of passive-aggressive comments or the carefully managed flow of information. The evolving SE goes into an account *expecting* office politics to affect the decision process. It is usually only a matter of time until they emerge.

Many factors drive individuals to engage in counter-productive office politics. Some office politics motivators include employees wanting to *avoid*:
  · Being labeled as boat rockers or troublemakers
  · Seeing others succeed, especially those they do not like or harbor jealousy towards
  · Missing out on promotion opportunities
  · Being embarrassed in front of others
  · Losing their jobs
  · Losing value or power (such as not being the only one with certain knowledge)

Some of these factors are driven by corporate culture. Others are initiated by the individual. Either way, these and other drivers will define the intensity of the politics that the SE must accept and navigate.

Office Politics Assessment Checklist

Think of a current client you have some working knowledge of and check off the statements that you believe reflect reality within their organization.

- ❏ Rarely are problems fully resolved
- ❏ Meetings frequently end without decisions or action items
- ❏ The same people get blamed, often with little evidence
- ❏ People do not discuss obvious problems
- ❏ There are conflicting cross-departmental goals
- ❏ Humor is often cynical and "back-stabbing"
- ❏ The more powerful the person, the more they take advantage of breaking rules, missing deadlines, etc. without apology
- ❏ People get quieter when a manager enters the room
- ❏ People eat lunches at their desks and rarely gather in common areas
- ❏ People frequently huddle in hallways and speak in low tones
- ❏ Less powerful people are treated with less respect
- ❏ It is obvious that associating with or being friendly with certain people is viewed upon as positive or negative
- ❏ Information is hoarded
- ❏ People rarely discuss their personal lives
- ❏ Constructive disagreement is frowned upon
- ❏ "Big picture" questions are rarely asked such as, *"What is our goal here?"* or *"How will that affect the long-term strategy?"*
- ❏ People do not give up their resources or agendas purely for the good of others
- ❏ People sit quietly at meetings and then complain afterwards about decisions that were made

STRATEGIES

In terms of analyzing the assessment, there is no magic number of checked items to look for in order to come up with a definitive conclusion regarding the political intensity of your client's organization. However, while many of the check listed items are present in all companies, in critical mass they are tell-tale signs of relatively political organizations.

This analysis is certainly not limited to the business world in its application. Neighborhood associations, religious groups, school committees and social clubs are likely to share these traits. While there are no easy answers when dealing with office politics, here are some strategies worth trying.

In a politically-dominated environment:

· **Observe the reality**

Every company has a mission statement proudly proclaiming why everyone is there. I remember sitting in on one meeting, chuckling to myself, as two managers basically fought over who would get the most recognition at an upcoming sales kick-off. Above them was a poster of 10 men in a row boat, rowing away, with the catchy quote, *"It is the ability to work together which determines success."*

Once you have seen the mission statement and heard about the higher business purpose, look behind the poster and see how things really get done:
  · Do they encourage dissent?
  · Does an employee have to be there a certain amount of time to have any influence?

- How regular and honest is communication down the ladder?
- How much time do managers spend debating, negotiating and protecting their turf vs. producing results?

✳✳

One client of ours was a classic case of do one thing, say another. On one hand, the executive level communicated to the population that contrasting viewpoints were welcomed. In fact, their survival was dependant on challenging each other's assumptions. This type of assertive, push-back behavior was widely publicized as tolerated and encouraged.

On some levels this appeared to be true. Particularly at the R&D level, meetings would frequently become contentious. The engineering team seemed totally comfortable engaging and challenging each others' ideas. It didn't seem to matter what the topic was or the title of the presenter—every idea was fair game. At the end of the day, excellent ideas arose from the ashes and people were pretty good at not taking it personally.

The director level was a different story. There appeared to be a unique, unspoken set of rules for directors. These people acted like sergeants in the army. They were there to execute orders from the VPs. No discussions, no debates, just compliance. If you were a director and understood this, you could do very well with the company. However, those who didn't get it, or genetically could not stop themselves from engaging in hearty debates, simply did not last long. I watched a consistent pattern emerge of candid, outspoken directors disappear based on excuses to get rid of them such as sudden organizational changes and rewriting of job descriptions.

As an evolving SE, the ability to see what is real in terms of office politics becomes an important survival skill. If you were in the previously mentioned company, challenging others at the engineering level would have been appropriate, however, when interacting with VPs and above, you would be best served by complying, not debating with their wishes. Yes, you can gain respect by voicing your opinion, but in this example, you would need to pick your battles carefully or you would find executive access no longer available and a generally diminished enthusiasm for your input.

· **Do not publicly embarrass or praise**
Embarrassing others in front of their peers has ten times the impact as embarrassing them privately. In a politically-dominant organization, surely this goes up even higher. Often the embarrassment is unintentional. But if the person is embarrassed, intent is not relevant. This is similar to an interviewer in the U.S.A. innocently asking a candidate, *"You have an interesting accent. Where are you from?"* Intent does not matter, the law has been broken.

Here are statements and questions that an SE might make or ask during a presentation at a **highly political** customer's site that could unintentionally embarrass the other party or cause a politically uncomfortable situation:

> · *"Jane, have you finished that project you were working on? I remember you were hitting some real obstacles the last time we talked."*

- *"Who's making the final call on this one?"*
- *"Steve, I know you're new and this is a pretty complex solution. Would you like me to explain it one more time?"*
- *"I have to tell you, I find your website a little confusing."*

Even **praising** someone publicly in a political environment is dangerous. For example, what if another employee who thinks that they are more deserving of praise is in the meeting? And what if both employees report to the same manager who is in the meeting? Jealousy and resentment may result, so, in general, only praise **group** efforts in public and save the **individual** praising for private.

- **Ask for more off-line opinions**

In a political environment people will hesitate to share their true feelings. Asking, *"What do you really think about this direction?"* will be met with silence from everyone except the most powerful people in the room. If you really do want others' opinions, elicit those opinions off-line and you are guaranteed to achieve better results.

- **Do not press for immediate decisions**

In highly political companies, people cannot be rushed into decisions. They will feel a need to consider all possible ramifications before feeling good about making a commitment. If you come from a fast-moving, energetic background, this can be very frustrating. Decisions that you believe should be made in hours may take days, or even weeks. You will wonder, *"Why can't they just make a decision? It's obvious what they need to do."* Maybe what's best for one department is obvious to you, but is extremely threatening to another. Without knowing what all the underlying agendas are, it is challenging to be patient. Pressuring others for quick decisions in this environment will not work and position you as problematic to those who require more time to think.

· **Do not discuss your personal life if they don't**
Cultures at some companies simply do not encourage discussions of a personal nature. This is almost always a top-down phenomenon. If a CEO talks about his or her personal life with peers and in a group setting, this usually results in others following suit. The closed-door executive who only reads prepared speeches, delivers meaningless corporate platitudes and makes no attempt to connect with those beneath him or her will often be surrounded with similar personality and style types. The effect trickles down from there and leads to a relatively sterile, cool culture.

The goal here for the SE is not to judge or try to change the environment. The goal is to assess and adjust. If the environment is "strictly business" then the SE should behave accordingly. The evolving SE knows that culturally fitting in is far more effective in a highly political environment than behaving naturally if the SE possesses a different social style.

I have heard many stories over the years involving SEs who struggle with this concept. I remember one SE telling me that he was just a naturally funny guy who could not help but be extremely outgoing and joke around whenever an opportunity arose. Often this involved mentioning something from his personal life or poking fun at someone at the client's site. He believed that customers understood and accepted this behavior because, "*Hey, that's just the way I am.*"

You have heard the phrase that we are our own worst critics. Sometimes I think the opposite is true. Often, we do not truly understand how others perceive us. Most of us believe that we are liked by others—the ego is a strong mechanism. It can be very challenging to realize that our style might create friction and not be welcomed by clients if it is incongruent with their political environment. Reading and then mirroring the client's political make-up is an important and highly valuable SE skill set.

Just imagine that on Monday morning you are giving a presentation to a client group. The culture is very cool and impersonal. You have concluded that office politics dominate the clients' actions. You walk into the room and half the people are working on email and the other half are debating the merits of a new marketing campaign. No one is smiling.

You had a great weekend and are in an excellent mood. You want this to be a collaborative, fun session so you decide to begin like this:

"Good morning, everyone. It's great to be here although I have to admit it was hard getting out of bed this morning. Yesterday I took my son skiing for the very first time. He did great and was so excited that he kept us up all night. So, let's maybe get one or two weekend stories from you all before I jump into the heavy stuff. Who did something really fun that they'd like to share with the group?"

Ouch. Great intent but a bad read. Your question is likely to be met with uncomfortable silence. In this political environment, it's critical to fight your instincts and behave in a manner that increases the group's comfort level with your behavior and style.

- **Do not initiate activities outside of work, unless invited**
  Similar to the previous point, if a client's employees do not socialize with each other outside of work, then you should not expect to either. In addition to behaving inconsistently with the client's culture, you run the added risk of being perceived as "too close" to the other party. It may seem petty but in highly political companies people will notice who you choose to see outside of work and form judgments. Likely statements and questions raised in political environments include:

  - *"Why did he take her to lunch? I've done all the work on this project."*
  - *"I heard the SE is taking Steve to the ball game. I can only imagine what Steve is going to tell him."*
  - *"I can't believe she is taking the Director of Marketing to lunch. Marketing never cooperates with us."*

This point about avoiding outside socializing inevitably leads to spirited debates during our workshops. The counter-argument is that seeing someone socially outside of the normal work environment is a great way to build relationships and better understand office politics.

If you really feel like the benefits of initiating such activities outweigh the potential downsides, then some flexibility is acceptable. But if you are going to initiate socializing outside of work, here is one more warning for your consideration.

Keep your socializing in the daylight.

Strange things happen after dark. Going out for dinner or other night time activities can be great relationship builders but there are consequences worth considering. You should certainly be on the lookout for these potential scenarios if you do choose to socialize after hours.

The client may want to:
- Drink excessive amounts of alcohol
- Expect you to drink
- Get your opinion on taboo topics, like religion or politics
- Go somewhere later in the night that would make you uncomfortable
- Stay out much later than you want to stay out
- Express feelings on non-business topics that truly offend you and will be difficult to ignore when back on the job

In addition you might make an innocent comment on a topic that they feel passionate about and take offense to. But, if you still feel compelled to engage in after-hours socializing, proceed with caution.

- **Elicit more input before meetings regarding agenda items**
This technique is recommended to avoid being thrown off-track by "surprise" agendas at meetings. In highly political environments, people will often come to

meetings with their own agendas and reveal those agendas after the meeting is well underway.

By eliciting input before the meeting, you have two added benefits:
1.   People are more likely to comment on or add to the agenda during the private nature of a pre-meeting communication with you.
2.   This allows you to use the agenda as the "bad guy" if the meeting goes off track.

To the second point, I highly recommend that you post the agenda in the meeting room where everyone can see it. Often the agenda is on a slide but if it is posted and someone tries to change the agenda during the meeting, simply point to the posted agenda and say something like:

"That's an interesting point, Jan, unfortunately as you can see on our agenda (point to agenda) we may not have time for that today. I'll make a note of your thought and let's come back to it later if we have time."

One key is to say *"if we have time"* not *"when we have time."* *"When"* implies an expectation and commitment to address the point during the presentation. *"If"* implies we are aware of your point and will try to get to it, but no commitments are involved.

·   **Be more attentive to copying emails to potentially affected parties**
Witnesses can be valuable! If you deal with someone who has "selective memory," copy emails to others who logically should be included in the loop. By doing this,

the other party will know that you have witnesses and be more likely to remember agreements and commitments.

One warning is to only send copies to truly affected parties. Copying an email, for example, to someone's manager (who has no great need to know about a particular action item) will obviously be insulting and destructive. It's best to tell the other party in advance who you will be copying the email to and why to avoid conflict and ill will.

Example:
"Terry, this sounds great. Steve was asking when he'll be needed so I'll summarize what we've come up with and send you and Steve an email later today."

· **Gain clarity on goals and success criterion before beginning projects**
There are bound to be conflicting goals and priorities in any company. In political companies, changing goals and success criterion, often half way through a project, is common. For example, you may be told initially that speed is the number one buying criterion, only to be told later that quality cannot be compromised. Something has to give.

While gaining agreement on goals and success criterion may prove difficult, there are few downsides in trying. By vigilantly asking thought provoking questions to the real decision makers (see Chapter 6 on *Mapping Client Organizations*) you will gain some clarity on how decisions will be made. The effort certainly beats blindly investing significant time and resources, only to be derailed well into the project by conflicting agendas.

- **Befriend management**
  Follow the money.

Yes, when in doubt, follow the money. Sometimes a political culture forces you to choose sides. Whose position are you going to support? Whose needs are you going to prioritize above the others? Whose confidant will you choose to be? The answer is, follow the money. Figure out who has the power to sign the check, draw a straight line down from him or her and you have your roadmap.

This may come off as a bit shallow and callous. But ask any of your top-performing account managers about this suggestion and you'll probably get a quick laugh followed by strong confirmation that every member of a sales team should absolutely follow this advice. If you are not sure how to follow the money in a specific account, ask your AM. Chances are excellent that he/she will be able to provide you with the answer.

- **Assure confidentiality on sensitive topics**
  People like to confide in outside, trusted sources, like you. The field of psychiatry is dependent on people valuing the objective, professional input of someone outside of their daily routines. Have you ever felt like a psychiatrist with one of your clients? If so, that's a good sign! That means that he/she trusts you enough to vent real feelings and is open to your objective input.

One guideline to facilitating this kind of relationship is to assure the other party of the confidential nature of any given conversation. When people hear your assurances they do not have to guess, assume, or worry later about others learning about your discussion.

Here's an example of a simple statement that will go a long way in gaining valuable information in a political environment:

"Raj, I wanted to ask you a question about your decision process. I also want you to know that anything we talk about is just between you and me. Okay? Great - thank you. It seems like three out of the four managers really like our ideas but I cannot seem to figure out why I can't win over Tammy. I know that you've stated your support for us, so I was curious if you had any suggestions."

This assurance of confidentiality is useful in many client situations, but in a politically charged environment it carries particular weight.

· **Put more in writing**

This harkens back to earlier comments regarding selective memory. In political organizations people are more likely to change their minds as they contemplate how commitments impact them personally vs. the company. By putting more in writing people clearly feel an enhanced sense of obligation. Also, you will be protecting yourself later if disagreements over action items occur. Similar to copying others on emails, it's best to have a reasonable position to share as to why you are putting items in writing in order to maintain collaborative feelings.

In a less politically-dominated environment:

· **Encourage constructive debate**

> *"When two men in business always agree,*
> *one of them is unnecessary."*
> William Wrigley, US chewing gum industrialist
> (1861-1932)

We have witnessed many examples in corporations around the world of the consequences of people not feeling free to disagree or raise hard issues.[1] This can result in the self-destructive, slow-burning downward spiral suffered by the US auto industry in the 1960s or the spectacular bubble-bursting demise of Enron in 2004. Research in Motion (RIM) and HP struggle with this as well as this book is being written.

Corporate cultures that allow their people to safely challenge each others' ideas, directions and actions are healthy, innovative places to work. Creative breakthroughs and corporate "reinvention" become possible by enabling this environment. Current leaders here include Facebook, Twitter and VMware.

For example, if you have been with a technology company for more than three years, chances are good that today's product is very different than the product you originally were introduced to and trained on. Maybe the basic function is the same but how it gets there is quite different.

Now, imagine that your product had never been updated and it is exactly the same as the day you arrived.

Where would your company be today? The best you could hope for is that your product is so unique that you are able to survive on its niche market share. More likely, the competition passed you long ago, your market share is steeply descending and you are losing or have lost your best talent. Unless your product is so generic that upgrades are not required (Q-Tips, Kleenex, etc.), your success today is the result of your ability to internally, constructively debate long term visions and short term decisions.

In a less political environment, this is a process that the evolving SE encourages. Make it your goal to build an image as one who enjoys having their ideas debated and challenged. Show curiosity and genuine enthusiasm when the client questions your recommendations. Learn the facilitation skills that will keep these discussions on a productive track and lead to the co-creation of value.

Examples of language that keep debates on a constructive track include:

"You say you don't like that idea, Tom. Tell me where you see the potential problems."

"I really feel like this is your best option but I can tell that most of you disagree with me, which is fine. Talk me out of it! What would you recommend and why?

"First, thanks for your candor. The only way that we're going to come up with a direction that you're going to embrace is if you let us know when you disagree."

When people disagree, they sometimes become very assertive in stating and holding their position ("*No,*

I'm SURE it won't work."). This tends to happen when people are tired, the meeting has gone on too long, there are personality conflicts, a personal need has not been identified or office politics are at play. Because we are now talking about strategies for a relatively *less* political environment, I would recommend that you try the approach of **encouraging the parties to seek one more option.**

Let them know that each of their ideas has merits. Then say something like, *"We have three potential directions. Let's try to come up with just one more option."* They will moan and groan. They might initially even become more defensive around their ideas. But after only a few minutes, you will be pleasantly surprised at the results. Hopefully they will come up with a new idea, but if not, at least they will be approaching the situation as a shared problem. There is almost always one more option to consider and it's incumbent on you to motivate the others to believe in the validity of this process and then facilitate the breakthrough.

· **Discuss personal lives**
The opposite of our warning in political environments, here you are encouraged and have the freedom to engage the client at a personal level. This is not an obligation but an option that should be exercised to the extent that you and the client feel comfortable.

Let's say, for example, that you run into one of your client's programmers, David, on Monday morning. After a simple *"How was your weekend, David?"* he gives you an extended, personal story about his family, including many personal details about his life. This should be viewed as an invitation for you to reciprocate. By sharing personal data about yourself you are telling David that *"I'm like you"* in terms of personality and social styles. This can make a big difference later on if David is contemplating confiding in you on more pressing matters.

Even when discussing personal lives there are limits to be aware of. I would still discourage you from initiating discussions regarding politics, religion, sex or other cultural taboos. If they want to talk about these topics, listen attentively, be polite but be very careful about voicing strong opinions. Acknowledgment is different than agreement.

· **Praise others publicly**
Again on the flipside to earlier warnings, much can be gained from publicly praising others in a less political environment. When done sincerely and with good reason, the receiver of the public praise will be far more impacted than you might suspect. Think about the last time a presenter specifically noted your contributions in front of a group. You probably felt a little embarrassed, followed by pride, gratitude and maybe even a desire to reciprocate.

In fact, if the environment is devoid of office politics, public praise might be an *expected* behavior. By not publicly acknowledging outstanding performances you might run the risk of disappointing those who believe they deserve credit and are waiting for it. A good example of this would be if a client's engineer spent significant time helping you synthesis complex data for a presentation. Ignoring this could hurt your chances for such cooperation next time. Instead, a simple, *"I want to thank Jan for spending so much time making sure I got this right,"* is all that it would take to set up the next successful joint effort.

· **Press harder for decisions**

When teams do not require significant time to mull over the ramifications of decisions, an SE should encourage faster decision making. SEs will deal mainly with technical team members whose tendency may be to over analyze issues that do not merit or require such scrutiny. This leads to the common analysis/paralysis trap, wasting time and resources. While the intent may be devoid of politics and underlying agendas, the results can still be a slowing down or stifling of the sales process.

Instead, encourage action. Don't push for decisions that others clearly are not ready to make or support, but feel free to impose "soft" deadlines to keep the momentum going. One technique to encourage this behavior is to state your intentions at the beginning of the meeting. A key is to include a reasonable position as to why others should share your goal regarding taking action.

"We've all done a lot of work gathering data so the goal for today's meeting is to decide whether or not to proceed with the PoC. **In order to meet the implementation deadlines that we agreed upon last month** *we need to decide today. Is everyone okay with that?"*

· **Hold more spontaneous, less formal meetings**

When the organization is less political, people are quite comfortable with spontaneous, less formal meetings. Here are examples of contrasting reactions you might receive based on the client's culture:

Highly political:

SE: *"Jan, could you join some of us from the technical group in the conference room in 30 minutes? We'd like to get your input on something."*

Jan: *"I have a pretty busy morning, how long will this take?"*

SE: *"About half an hour."*

Jan: *"What are we going to discuss?"*

SE: *"The status of the demonstration and what to do as next steps."*

Jan: *"Who's going to be there?"*

SE: *"Juan, Terry and Robin."*
Jan: *"Why is Terry there? I thought she was off the evaluation committee."*

SE: *"She still has more knowledge on the system than anyone else."*

Jan: *"I still don't see why Terry should join us for this meeting. I'll attend and I'm certainly glad to listen, just don't count on me for a lot of input. Also, I won't be able to make any decisions until I talk to my manager."*

Less political:

SE: *"Jan, could you join some of us from the technical group in the conference room in 30 minutes? We'd like to get your input on something."*

Jan: *"What's the meeting about and how long will it take?"*

SE: *"We're going to discuss the status of the demonstration and what to do as next steps. It should take about half an hour."*

Jan: *"Sure, I'll see you there. Also, feel free to invite Terry or anyone else you think might have valuable input."*

- **Hold more brainstorming sessions**
One final recommendation for the less political environment is to hold more brainstorming sessions. Brainstorming sessions work when people can collaborate in an unfettered, free-wheeling atmosphere. As soon as participants begin to edit what they say or analyze the ideas of others, the spontaneity and effectiveness of the session is lost. It is the responsibility of the SE to make these sessions "safe" for all to participate fully.

Although there is some overlap, facilitating brainstorming sessions takes different skills and behaviors than generally required for traditional facilitation efforts. Be sure that if you are considering a training class for yourself on facilitation skills that it includes a specific component on brainstorming sessions.

****

In summary, your job as an SE is not to fix or change your client's office politics. Your job is to *assess* the political landscape and then *behave* in ways that the environment dictates will be most productive. By situationally following the guidelines in this chapter you will find yourself a welcomed guest of your clients' organizations and a sought after confidant and resource for those involved in the buying process.

(1) On November 3, 2004, A jury convicted a former Enron Corp. executive and four ex-Merrill Lynch & Co. officials in the first criminal prosecution arising from the accounting fraud that led to the energy trader's collapse. On December 8, 2000, Enron was named one of the "100 Best Companies to Work For in America" by Fortune magazine.

Chapter 9

KEEPING ACCOUNT MANAGERS HAPPY

A s alluded to in this book's introduction, account managers **own** their accounts. They will receive credit when things go well and blame when things don't. They will be on top of the world one quarter, driving up in their brand new BMWs, and on the phone the next quarter, begging for a quota-making deal. It's important for SEs to understand that this rollercoaster defines an AM's existence.[1]

Although most sales engineers today have some monetary bonus linked to regional performance, the percentage of their income that is tied to sales figures is relatively low. Also, if a region is not making its numbers, it is highly unlikely that the SE will take the heat. It's usually the salesperson who is put "on plan" and will eventually be "reallocated" if improvement is not forthcoming. Most sales engineers look at money tied to sales as a bonus, while account managers look at this money as their bread and butter.

Occasionally I will hear sales engineers express resentment and jealousy regarding account manager compensation. SEs sometimes feel like they are doing all the heavy lifting and deserve more. They lament that their AMs just sit in the back of the room while the SE explains the technology and sells its benefits. I've heard many SEs make statements such as, *"In reality, I do all the selling."*

Whenever I hear SEs going down this road I like to ask them this question:

"Yes, it sounds like the AMs have it made here. Have you thought about becoming an AM?"

The predictable smile is usually followed by a statement such as:

"Yes, but I just don't like the selling part of it."

To better understand the real reasons behind their reticence to becoming account managers, I spoke with a very experienced, Senior SE. He told me:

> *"Sales engineers are morbidly afraid of a variable paycheck. They just don't have the stomachs that the sales reps do when it comes to living on the edge. They want that paycheck to be the same or more every time. They just cannot deal with it being less in the 'lean quarters.'*
>
> *They see the sales reps tortured by sales management when they miss the mark, and yet somehow they [the sales engineers] receive little heat regarding failures. They have a pretty insulated status when it comes to poor performance by the region."*

It's important and healthy that as an evolving SE

169

you respect what it takes to succeed as an AM. By appreciating how challenging and all-consuming their jobs are you will be more open to contributing to their success. You will also be more accepting of what occasionally seem like unwarranted or extreme demands.

That's not to say that SEs should surrender to every AM request. Part of your work should be to establish guidelines and precedence for working together. Most account managers like it when their SEs make special requests or attempt to negotiate action items, assuming that there is an acceptable justification that will benefit the sales effort.

One example was offered by John, a participant in one of our workshops. He shared with the group that he was getting frustrated by being constantly told by one of his account managers to show up to do demonstrations with almost no background information being provided about the client.

He sat down with this account manager to discuss a different approach. John showed the AM how he could link their technology to specific job functions during a presentation. He then provided an example of how this approach with another client had resulted in a large purchase with a relatively shorter sales cycle.

John and the account manager agreed that in the future the account manager would ask the client for the job functions that would be in attendance and forward that information to John. This simple agreement has resulted in wins for John, the account manager and the clients who, from that day forward, have enjoyed far more tailored and on-target presentations.

Keeping your AMs happy should not be difficult. It is based on establishing a foundation of empathy and mutual respect. Three guidelines to facilitate the building of this foundation are:

1. Only discuss future products with AM approval

*"You think this is good,
I hear the next version is going to be amazing."*
Anonymous **Un-evolved** SE

Everything you do should be within the context of driving revenue, unless told otherwise. Discussing future products will usually have the opposite effect. If you were the customer and heard the quote above, what would you do? Clearly, you would think that the new version sounds great and, barring any emergency needs for the current product, tell the account manager that you have decided to wait a while. Ouch! Now there's a long ride back to the office for the SE!

Here is a question that is sure to elicit laughter from a class of SEs: *"Have you ever had a product release date slip?"* It would probably be easier to count the number of release dates that have occurred on schedule. Plus, even if the release is on time, there are bound to be bugs or other product surprises that will cause prospects to pause before committing. So, even if your next version or upgrade is going to be available soon, avoid alluding to it until you have obtained clearance from your account manager.

There are two situations that merit the mentioning of future products. They are:

- **When the relationship is strategic and the client needs to be assured that your development direction aligns with theirs.**

- **When you are in danger of losing a deal to the competition because their products have features that yours lack, but your company is currently developing those very features or similar ones that will meet the client's needs.**

Tell your account manager if either of these is true regarding a sale you are working on together. Then strategize on how to mention future products in ways that either align you strategically with the client's direction or stymie the competition.

2. Present to business drivers

Here is one of those areas that can really help you stand out as a superstar with your account manager. It also an area that just about every SE claims to understand but precious few apply in the real world. This guideline requires you to connect your company's technology with the client's stated business goals.

The first example below would be considered technically accurate but lacking the desired business connection. The second example is more of what I would expect to hear from an evolving SE.

Example #1
Technology driven

"As you can see, our software will really help your business. Because it is standards based, you will be able to much more easily configure, deploy and maintain. Far fewer resources are required for building robust applications. A lot of your web based applications will be easy to build, thanks to the development environment."

Example #2
Business driven

"Earlier you mentioned your need to cross-departmentally share data in an effort to reduce redundancies and overall costs of operation. Our standards based software is designed to allow your current silos of data to be shared between departments and help you achieve that goal, as you've shared is so important for Steve's team in support and Jenna's marketing team. For example, let's say that one of your salespeople in the insurance vertical has a question regarding a customer's open support ticket..."

The second example just jumps off the page and grabs the audience's attention. The SE barely mentions technology but is scoring big points by showing tremendous sensitivity and knowledge about the compelling business needs driving the sale. Notice also that the SE ends by giving a client-specific example of how the solution would work in the client's day-to-day operations.

When AMs see sales engineers presenting to business drivers they are usually pleasantly surprised, if not shocked. You have now relieved the account manager of the burden of making what could be tricky connections between the technology (which you so thoroughly understand) and the client's needs. Also, because you are showing your knowledge of both the business and technical challenges your explanation of the solution will carry more credibility with the client.

The examples given are dependent on the audience and its expectations. A purely technical group, say of programmers, might find the first example more compelling. As you work with higher levels and mixed audiences, the second example becomes more effective and appropriate.

3. Develop consistent planning habits

Evolving SEs are proactive when it comes to planning with their account managers. They attempt to strategize with their AMs before every customer interaction. John provided us with an excellent example of a productive planning conversation earlier in this chapter. Obtaining buy-in from AMs for future planning sessions occurs when they see and hear the results you produce because of previous team planning.

When you ask AMs for information during your planning, it is important that you leverage that information when interacting with clients. Avoid requesting "nice-to-know" data, obtained out of general curiosity or personal interest. **Then be sure to display the value of your joint planning whenever your AMs join a meeting or presentation.** Seeing is believing, and, when you think about it, as an SE you are really engaged in an ongoing effort to sell your value to your clients *and* account managers.

In our workshop, *Consultative Essentials for Sales Engineers*, we provide a full joint call planner for participant post-workshop use. Here are a few examples of questions from that planner that might be useful for you to ask your AM in preparation for a client meeting:

- What's presently occurring at their company that has motivated them to now consider changing technologies?
- What are the titles of the attendees?
- What, if any, information should I not share with the client?
- What would have to happen in this meeting for the client and you to consider the meeting a success?

Some other areas that might be important to explore include the competition, budget, and the client's decision process. Notice how the sample questions above are open-ended, to elicit lengthier, richer responses.

JOINT CALL MISTAKES

Over the last 15 years Technically Speaking has heard and documented joint call stories ranging from the impressive to the disastrous. Having a partner with you on a joint call should be an advantage. You have twice as many ears to listen with and twice as many minds with which to think. Read the list that follows. It contains many of the most common joint call mistakes made. Check off the ones that you have personally seen or experienced. Then mentally lock them away in your "*Not to do*" list on future joint calls.

Joint Call Mistakes

- Unclear call success criterion for SE/AM team and client
- No discussion regarding what information **not to share** with client
- Unclear timeframe for each agenda item
- No discussion about the dress code or formality level of meeting
- No planning on how to answer typical, predictable objections
- Unclear on who will summarize and close the call
- Assumptions regarding who is responsible for bringing what materials
- Talking over each other
- Poor transitions from one person to the next
- Surprising partner by tossing them a difficult question ("Hot potato" vs. "hand-off")
- One party dominating
- Both parties dominating—loss of customer involvement
- Use of *"I"* vs. *"We"*
- Disagreeing or debating with partner
- Concessions without partner's consent
- Lack of supportive nonverbal behaviors towards each other

✱✱✱

In summary, keeping your account managers happy is a giant step forward in your evolution and should be a top priority. Earning their trust and respect will be a key contributor to team success and personal job satisfaction. If you are able to stay focused on currently available products, talk to business drivers during client meetings, develop a consistent planning process, and avoid typical joint call mistakes, you will be delighted by your account manager's reaction and the benefits to you that will follow.

We will now transition to the behavioral, tactical section of the book and focus on *interpersonal* techniques. You will find that these are extremely practical and readily applicable to both solo and joint call opportunities.

(1) According to Harvey Bass, president and managing director of the Sparta, N.J., office of Sales Consultants International, a recruiting firm based in Cleveland, Ohio, *"The average tenure of a new salesperson is 12 to 24 months because this industry [technology] is so volatile and entrepreneurial."* Source, Kelloggforum.org website, 2008. (http://www.kelloggforum.org/careers-in-technology-sales/)

TACTICAL ESSENTIALS

INTRODUCTION

I n this section we move from the strategic to the tactical. Here you will learn specific techniques and communication recommendations for being more productive and persuasive when directly interacting with clients and team members. On their own, each idea is useful but when combined and consistently applied, they will result in you exuding a formidable presence, guaranteed to shape highly desirable and powerful impressions.

These ideas are applicable to SEs worldwide. While cultural differences always need to be considered they have been taught and accepted on a global scale.

By the end of this section you will know how to:
- Maintain a desirable airtime ratio between you and your client
- Professionally begin a discovery process
- Ask questions designed to enhance your image
- Make appropriate personal appearance and wardrobe decisions
- Plan what to ask and when to ask it
- Plan what to say and what not to say

- Choose between communicating via email, the phone, or face to face
- Structure a presentation for maximum impact and persuasiveness
- Place and keep the focus on you vs. your slides during presentations
- Uncover the personal needs of others that often drive decision making
- Embrace change

In addition, each technique is highly collaborative in nature. SEs often can choose different paths for reaching their goals. While each of these choices may be equally successful, the impact of these choices on relationships is worth considering. For example, if you cannot obtain satisfactory cooperation from your main point of contact at a client's site, you might call his or her manager and voice your concern. This may result in an increased level of cooperation from your contact but a diminished level of overall support. The ideas in this section consider these issues and take the "high road," applying techniques designed to maintain excellent long-term relationships with all client contacts.

As we have touched on earlier, in addition to clients, you are frequently selling yourself to account managers, your manager and other team members. The ideas in this section will be applicable to these relationships as well, increasing the quality of the communications you experience with your colleagues and their level of trust in you. Results will include greater autonomy, increased professional respect and elevated status within the team.

The first chapter in this section addresses airtime ratio, a topic that is usually given little attention yet merits serious discussion. Have you ever thought about what percentage of the time SEs should be talking as compared to their customers? Evolving SEs are sensitive to this issue and aware of its impact on the sale. Read on—the answer might surprise you!

Chapter 10

MAINTAIN A PROPER AIRTIME RATIO

Over the duration of a sales cycle, what percentage of the time do you think the SE should be talking as compared to the customer? When we pose this question to class participants, we usually get politically correct answers like, *"The SE should talk about 30% of the time."* Then we ask participants to tell us what they estimate the percentage really is out in the field? After a few chuckles and some silence, we tend to hear some pretty honest answers like, *"Okay, we talk about 70% of the time!"*

So what is the right answer? How much should you be talking? There are two answers. One is, *"It depends,"* and the other answer is, *"50%."*

The *"It depends"* answer is related to how far along the deal is in the sales cycle. At the beginning of the sales cycle (the first meeting or two), SEs should be listening significantly more than talking. This is the time for gathering data and gaining insight into the client's preferences, expectations and goals, also known as "PEGs." At this early stage, SEs cannot possibly know enough to describe their products and services in ways that will be meaningful to their clients. When SEs talk more than clients early in the sales cycle, the client may be polite but internally is probably experiencing some level of boredom or frustration.

Clients often, unknowingly, encourage an undesirable airtime ratio. They ask SEs to come in and talk about technology while they passively listen. They believe that watching a corporate presentation will tell them what they need to know about a product and answer their major questions. These clients often start meetings by telling SEs to *"just give us an overview of what your solution does."* Often this process is relayed through account managers who tell their SEs to *"just do the usual demo."*

Evolving SEs know that this scenario is a losing proposition for everyone. Without having an understanding of the client's business model and how technology will address specific issues, there is almost no chance that the presentation will be on target and create a compelling business case. As clients listen to this kind of generic presentation they will be simultaneously wondering how the product applies to their business. Because part of their attention is focused on building bridges between the demonstration and their company's needs, they are unable to give the SE 100% of their focus. Valuable information is likely to be missed. In addition, this constant need for bridge building by clients is draining and can turn a presentation into a mentally exhausting experience.

With higher level titles present (VPs and above) there is an even greater need to create bridges to their needs whenever discussing your products or services, as their pure interest in technology will usually be lower than others with whom you interact. Evolving SEs invest time to understand what issues are most important to the titles who will be in attendance. Examples of issues that resonant with executives include: ROI, branding, market share, scalability, uptime, CAPEX (capital expenditure) and OPEX (operational expenditure). By avoiding the trap of delivering a monologue early in the sales cycle (i.e. undesirable airtime ratio), you can uncover which executive needs are most material in the decision process and then design your strategy for satisfactorily addressing each.

The chart below shows the acceptable percentage of time that SEs should be doing the talking as they move through the sales cycle.

You can see that it is recommended that SEs do

AIRTIME RATIO

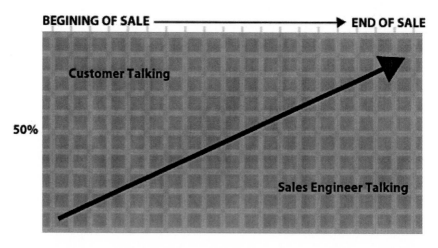

most of the talking as the sale nears closure. This is appropriate as SEs now understands how to connect their technology to the client's needs. Demonstrations and explanations become lengthier and more one sided, yet the client is fully engaged, enjoying hearing how the solution directly impacts their business. There is always the need for customer involvement but SEs should feel positive about taking up a larger percentage of the airtime later in the cycle.

The second answer, regarding how much SEs should be talking as compared to customers, was "50%." Notice that the chart supports this recommendation as well. While the ratio varies significantly at different points during the sales cycle, over the total duration of the cycle, airtime should be about equal for both parties.

One key to maintaining the proper airtime ratio is to pay special attention to how much you talk in the **first client meeting**. You may be tempted to violate our chart if the client sits back and asks you to, *"Tell me all about your product."* Or, if you are an SE who is most comfortable when talking about technology, you may be susceptible to talking too much during early encounters.

In our experience, on a global scale, SEs appear to be most comfortable when they are talking vs. listening. This makes sense for all professions. Everyone is naturally more at ease when discussing their area of expertise or core competency. As an SE you have the added tension of being in a sales role, so you naturally gravitate to behaviors that gives you a sense of comfort and security.

Reversing the airtime ratio may take a conscious effort to change, particularly if you're used to a reactive vs. proactive approach to customer interactions. Many SEs think that they are helping customers by waiting for questions and then giving technically accurate responses. Evolving SEs understand the philosophy of the airtime ratio chart and purposely act to maintain the desired balance.

****

In summary, adhering to the airtime ratio chart benefits everyone. You will save time by presenting only what is most relevant, your account manager will see deals closing quicker and customers will be freed of the burden of having to decipher, *"How exactly does this apply to us?"* In the next chapter you will learn a technique for gaining control of the sales conversation that will help promote a desirable airtime ratio and ultimately lead to richer and more meaningful conversations

Chapter 11

TEE UP THE CONVERSATION

Once we have established rapport with a client, it can sometimes be awkward or clumsy to move from *"How was your weekend?"* to the business at hand. Going beyond, *"What would you like to accomplish today?"* this transitional moment is a great opportunity to show the customer your organizational skills and let them know that you have done some serious preparation for the meeting.

✳✳

In golf, stepping up to the ball is known as "addressing" the golf ball. How difficult could that be? Here are some of the considerations when addressing a golf ball:
- Waist bend
- Knee bend
- Weight distribution between legs
- Distance to spread feet
- Ball position
- Shoulder angle
- Club grip

- Spine angle
- Chin position

If you have ever played golf you know that an infinite number of errors can occur during the swing. But at least by addressing the ball correctly you have put yourself in a position to succeed. It sets the direction you are planning to follow and gives you a sense of control and confidence. You will see the best golfers in the world still practicing their address position. Virtually every amateur golf lesson includes time devoted to address position.

****

Initiating a needs analysis is much like addressing a golf ball. We call this *"Teeing Up"* the conversation. By beginning with a professional and structured approach you will enjoy a sense of control and confidence. In addition you will be enhancing the customer's perception of your professionalism and increasing their interest in following your lead.

Here is the recommended three-step process for properly teeing up a client conversation. These steps are sequential, although there is some leeway allowed for personal style preferences.

- **Give a win/win reason**
- **Define the process**
- **Include time boundaries**

1. Give a win/win reason
This step means beginning the transition to the business at hand by sharing the benefits that both parties

will enjoy from engaging in the process that you are going to be recommending in Step #2, *Define the process*. Giving a win/win reason tees up the conversation properly and highlights the mutual value of moving forward. It also confirms the meeting's goals and gives the client a chance to share additional expectations.

In the earlier example, *"What would you like to accomplish today?"* there is no benefit given for what is to follow for either party. Instead, specifically state what is in it for you and the client, and then move to the next step.

Example:
*"Thanks for meeting with me today. **In order to make sure that I fully understand your goals for this initiative** (benefit to SE) **so that I can put together a proposal that covers all of your needs...**" (benefit to client)*

2. Define the process

Next, you should give a brief description of the *process* you would like to follow that will lead to the previously stated benefits that both parties will enjoy. Yes, both parties know that they are there to exchange information. However, to maintain control of **how** that exchange of information occurs, it is important to define the process. It might sound like this:

Example:
*"Thanks for meeting with me today. In order to make sure that I fully understand your goals for this initiative (benefit to SE) so that I can put together a proposal that covers all of your needs (benefit to client) **I've prepared a few questions that I'd like to ask you regarding your current and future growth goals."** (define the process)*

3. Include time boundaries

At this point the client will understand your recommended process for the meeting. This will give an increased sense of organization to the discussion. Because of today's time-sensitive business environment it is also important that you quickly and accurately set **time boundaries for** the questioning portion of your meeting:

Example:

*"Thanks for meeting with me today. In order to make sure that I fully understand your goals for this initiative (benefit to SE) so that I can put together a proposal that covers all of your needs (benefit to client) I've prepared a few questions I'd like to ask you regarding your current and future growth goals (define the process). **These questions should take no more than 10 minutes. Is that okay?"** (include time boundaries)*

As soon as clients hear how long the questions are expected to take, they relax. Let's say that your client only has 15 minutes for the meeting and instead of using the above example you just dive into your questions, as shown at the beginning of this chapter (*"What would you like to accomplish today?"*). What do you think would happen? Most likely, the client would politely answer your questions for the first few minutes but inside he or she might be wondering:

- *"How long are these questions going to take?"*
- *"When am I going to get to ask questions?"*
- *"How do I interrupt to let this SE know that I did not plan on answering questions for two-thirds of this meeting and that I have to leave in 15 minutes!"*

By announcing your time boundary and gaining acceptance to proceed, you give clients the opportunity to share their comfort or discomfort with your process. You should feel relieved, not rejected, if they tell you, *"I really don't have enough time for this right now."* Thank them for their candor. Let them know that these questions are important so it would be better for all parties to reschedule at a time when they can give you full attention and thoughtful responses.

This tee up technique has other benefits. For one, it helps you appear more consultative. When you apply this technique you will sense the difference in how clients react to you. You will be perceived as highly organized and professional. Because of this enhanced perception they will be more interested and willing to follow your recommended process.

In addition, this technique is useful for gaining or re-gaining control of the conversation. For example, have you ever walked into a room expecting one or two attendees and found yourself facing a room full of people? After barely getting out a *"Good morning"* they began bombarding you with questions or concerns. By allowing the group to take control you may never get your needs met and valuable time might be wasted on low priority topics.

Bankers Day

A few years ago, I was asked develop a training proposal for a local bank. In order to tailor my proposal, I set up a discovery meeting with the VP leading the initiative. I was only expecting the two of us. When I arrived, there were six bankers (all VPs) eagerly waiting for me.

After exchanging pleasantries and introductions, they launched into a barrage of questions for me to volley: "What do you know about loan processing?" "What makes you think that you'll succeed in a banking environment?" "What references can you provide that match our bank's model for customer service?" etc.

I politely answered the first few questions and then realized that this conversation was unproductive and spinning out of control. I also knew that this was the perfect time to wrestle back some control by using the tee up technique, so I addressed the group with this response:

"I'm happy to answer all of those questions today. In order for me to finish my proposal (benefit to SE) and make sure that it includes all of your needs (benefit to client) I've prepared a few questions that I'd like to ask you. These should take no more than 10 minutes for us to go through together (include time boundaries). Is that okay?"

The group agreed and I was allowed to ask my questions, taking back control of the meeting. The meeting went very smoothly and, interestingly enough, many of the questions that had initially been asked were not repeated. My guess is that the initial questions were designed to test my credibility, which apparently I established later on. By taking control using the tee up technique, the tone of the meeting became collaborative and organized, and we had a much more productive session as a result.

In the 15-plus years that I have been asking clients permission to ask them questions, I have <u>never</u> had a client say, *"No, that's not okay"* to my request. And if anyone ever did tell me that it was not okay, I would have to assume that they were not serious about us doing business together or I would need to dig further to understand their lack of enthusiasm for cooperating with such a reasonable request.

Smoothly and professionally delivering a tee up statement takes practice. In our classes, participants write out tee up statements and then practice delivering them to each other. We also recommend that participants write out tee up statements and refer to them when first using with customers. If not, it's too easy to forget one of the three steps that they should contain. Because this technique is just as useful over the phone, phone calls are great opportunities to practice tee up statements. Over the phone you can read your statements exactly as you have written them down without distracting the customer or appearing to be practicing a new skill.

EXCEPTION TO THE RULE

We *do not* recommend the tee up technique if the client called the meeting. In this case, they have a specific agenda and known goals that they are expecting you to help them address. Taking control right at the start would make little sense and result in you appearing far too controlling. After establishing rapport simply ask *"What would you like to accomplish today?"*

This does not mean that you have lost the opportunity to put some structure into the meeting. In a customer-initiated meeting the conversation might go like this:

195

Customer

"Thanks for coming in. We're looking to virtualize our systems and want to know how your company would approach such a complex project."

SE

"Of course. I'd be glad to share our approach. In order to make sure that I give you the right information for your company's goals, would it would be okay if I started by asking you a few questions that I've prepared. These should take no more than about 10 minutes?"

Customer

"You prepared questions? Okay. Go ahead."

Ah ha. Do you see what the SE just did? He/she is on the road to the desired airtime ratio detailed in Chapter 10. The SE is back in control of the conversation after allowing the customer to move in a different direction at first, as it was their meeting. One additional lesson here is that you should **always be prepared to deliver a tee up statement**. You never know where the conversation might head or who might be in the room so be ready to take control as needed.

✸✸

In summary, the tee up technique provides a smooth and professional way to begin, direct and redirect a sales conversation. In addition, it shapes the consultative perception desired by evolving SEs as being fully prepared for client meetings and committed to understanding their needs before delivering technical recommendations.

Once you have teed up the conversation and gained permission to ask questions of your clients, you have numerous options regarding what types of questions to ask them. In the next chapter you will learn about one category of questions that is frequently employed by evolving SEs.

Chapter 12

ASK THOUGHT-PROVOKING QUESTIONS

People judge you as much by the questions you ask as the answers you give.

During a needs analysis, what questions would you typically ask your clients?

Common SE answers include:
- *"What does your current system look like?"*
- *"How much traffic does your site handle?"*
- *"What other applications are you running?"*
- *"Who else will be involved in the evaluation?"*
- *"What are your worldwide needs?"*
- *"What would you like to accomplish with our software?"*

These are probably the same questions that clients have been asked internally and by every other vendor vying for their business. When this occurs, clients are likely to view the buying process as a necessary evil. They are forced to engage in duplicate conversations with multiple vendors with few, if any, tangible benefits to the clients outside of obtaining multiple proposals.

In addition, these questions only **passively** engage clients. They will give answers that they have given numerous times before, requiring minimal thought or energy on their part. The interaction becomes an interview, not a dialogue.

Not to minimize the value of this information, these kinds of questions are necessary. The hard data and metrics that these questions uncover are required to craft accurate proposals and recommend action steps. But evolving SEs understand the importance of asking questions that go beyond the mundane and predictable; to challenge the client to explore other important areas that require true introspection. These types of questions are called *"thought-provoking"* questions and they have many benefits.

By asking thought-provoking questions you will:
- Differentiate yourself and your company from the competition
- Send the message that your areas of interest go beyond the tactical, technical issues
- Increase the chances of you being invited to higher level, more strategic client meetings
- Gather richer information with which to leverage an advantage
- Change the buying process from passive to active by asking questions that require clients to more deeply consider their responses

Because most SEs have been trained in the use of open-ended questions, it is important to understand the distinction between open-ended and thought-provoking questions. Open-ended questions elicit lengthy responses; more than *"yes," "no,"* or other one word answers. Thought-provoking questions elicit lengthy responses as well, but in addition require customers to truly think before responding. Thought-provoking questions *cannot easily be answered by clients* because the answers will not come to them automatically. Even a question such as, *"What would you like to accomplish with our software?"*, while valuable, requires minimal thought or introspection. The client has probably given this question consideration and would not need additional time for analysis before answering.

A thought-provoking question requires the client to do one of the following:

- **Express a subjective opinion**
  "What's your opinion of the software so far?"

- **Look to the future**
  "How do you see your system evolving over time?"

- **Prioritize**
  "How would you rank the trade-off between speed and accuracy?"

How do you know when you have hit the target and asked a good, thought-provoking question? You will hear an answer similar to this one:

"Hmm, that's a good question, I've never thought about that before."

This is one of the most desirable responses that an SE can hope to hear. Here are some additional thought-provoking questions that other SEs have offered during our workshops. Notice how each requires the other party to; *express an opinion, look to the future, or prioritize.* The final question is directed at an account manager to make the point that these can be used internally as well:

- *"In a perfect world, how would you like to see our system impact your online operations?"*
- *"If you were to prioritize your architectural goals, what goals would be numbers one and two on that list and why?"*
- *"What do you believe your current systems do best?"*
- *"What systems should we be sensitive to maintaining as we migrate forward?"*
- *"How do we compare to other technologies that you're considering?"*
- *"What would your users say they like most and like least about navigating your portal?"*
- *"What is our measurement of success for this meeting?"* (to account manager)

It is challenging to come up with excellent, thought-provoking questions during client interactions, so prepare yours in advance. Many SEs have left meetings wishing to themselves, *"I should have asked him or her that."* By investing just a few minutes upfront, preparing thought-provoking questions that are situation-specific, evolving SEs enjoy the benefits detailed earlier, without the pressure of having to invent these questions in the moment.

It is acceptable and advisable to write them down and read them to make sure that you ask the questions correctly and elicit desired reactions. Clients won't mind if you read your questions word for word off a piece of paper. In fact, this works to your benefit by showing that you have gone the extra mile to prepare for this interaction and clients see that you have tailored your analysis expressly for them.

Another wonderful benefit to asking thought-provoking questions is that a client will feel like the questions have been written specifically to analyze his or her company. When written properly, they should sound very tailored. This leads to clients feeling an enhanced sense of importance to you and they are more likely to respond enthusiastically. In practice, you won't need to reinvent the wheel every time. You will most likely develop two or three thought-provoking questions that you will be able to successfully use with just about every client. You will find yourself consistently using these and minimize the need to invest significant time preparing new ones.

For example, at Technically Speaking we conduct numerous needs analysis interviews. We have found one question that ends interviews on such a thoughtful, positive note, that we use it with just about everyone.

"What would have to happen in this session for you and the group to feel like it was an excellent investment of their time?"

This question:
- Shows that we are *concerned about results*
- Sets the *success criterion* for the session
- Shows our *sensitivity to the cost* of taking SEs out of the field

****

In summary, SEs still need to ask traditional closed and open-ended questions to learn about customer requirements and needs. The evolving SE will go a step further, probing deeper and challenging the client to truly analyze their goals and priorities before responding. This will lead to the uncovering of richer, more detailed information while helping shape the SE's image as a strategic and thoughtful asset.

Chapter 13

LOOK EXPENSIVE

"*To establish yourself in the world a person must do all they can to appear already established.*"
La Rochefoucauld, Francois De, 1613-1680,
French Classical Writer

*L*ook expensive is one of those tips guaranteed to lead to lively discussion in our classes. Participants are bound to have different opinions regarding the definition of "expensive" and the global applicability of this advice. Clearly, there is room for diverse outlooks on the topic, but in this chapter you will learn why, overall, the concept is appropriate for SEs. Particularly in today's business-casual environment, it is challenging to make appearance decisions that are both comfortable for the SE and project the desired image to the client. So, while this is a highly subjective area, I will detail why looking expensive is usually a plus.

Should you be judged by what you wear? Perhaps not, but in reality you are. Without a deeper working knowledge of you, others are bound to formulate and hold opinions of you based on your appearance. The same is true for businesses in general. Whole companies are judged by the appearance of their office buildings and websites. Products often succeed or fail based solely on visual impact and packaging. Think of yourself as a product. Package yourself in ways that project success and confidence. Look like an SE who would be comfortable tackling mission critical issues and dealing with the highest of executive levels.

Take a look at some typical statements that we hear from SEs regarding appearance and assess how much you agree with each:

- *"I don't want to look like a salesperson."*
- *"I only dress up if a high level person is going to be in the room."*
- *"The technical people won't trust me if I get dressed up."*
- *"If the company is casual, I go casual."*

Each of these statements has merit and, situationally, could be argued persuasively. They also reflect the personal preference and experience of the SE delivering the statement. So while each has some validity, evolving SEs avoid using these as excuses for poor or mediocre personal presentation.

The most important question to consider is **what message do you want to send by your appearance?** In other words, what traits do you want the other party to believe you possess when you walk into the room?

An evolving SE you should be perceived as:
- Successful
- Neat and organized in your thinking
- A provider of a very high quality product
- Serious about your work and the importance of your job to your clients' success
- Respectful of the client/provider relationship
- Capable of interacting with higher levels

Notice that I use the word *expensive* in the title of this chapter. Why expensive? Simply put, because you, your company and your products *are* expensive. You represent a significant investment to your clients in terms of time, money and use of their resources. Your appearance should reflect and reinforce you and your product's cost and the high correlating value that both will bring to the client. A company making a significant investment is far more comfortable with a partner whose persona reflects their quality and proof of their ability to succeed. What would your first impression be of an investment consultant who showed up at your house in jeans and a wrinkled polo shirt?

This does not mean that SEs should be expected to go out and buy $5,000 Armani suits or lease Ferraris. With all the available fashion options out there, it is possible look expensive without spending a lot of money. You can look expensive by showing up to a casual meeting in a starched shirt and shined shoes. You can look expensive by wearing pressed black pants, a shiny leather belt, a starched, white button down shirt and a clean, stylish tie. Women can buy beautiful jewelry for a lot, or not so much money. You can look expensive by simply carrying a shiny leather portfolio instead of a beat up bike messenger bag. You *can* look expensive, even on a budget.

A police officer friend of mine told me that when officers approach someone on the street they look at the person's shoes for an immediate first impression of what they might be dealing with. One of the first purchasing agents I dealt with told me that the first thing he noticed about vendors was their shoes. He felt that their professional level and an excellent indicator of their success were their shoes.

Even with quality shoes, mistakes can happen. How about black shoes with brown pants or a broken lace that's been tied together like we used to do as kids? Other shoe-related mistakes happen with socks. I remember being in a meeting sitting next to a very well dressed SE. He was wearing a pair of dark blue, pressed wool slacks, a starched, white button down shirt and a new pair of black loafers. Unfortunately, when he crossed his legs he revealed a worn out pair of red socks decorated with baseballs! Maybe they think that's cute at the little league field but the client was not impressed.

Also, you never know who might be in the meeting. Let's say, for example, that you have an upcoming meeting with a team of programmers and developers. These folks rarely see the light of day and are notorious for showing up in shorts and T-shirts. Not wanting to offend them and wanting to blend in, you throw on some jeans and a T-shirt. You make sure the T-shirt is ironed but you still look like you're dressing for a day of classes at college.

The meeting is going great and the group really seems to accept you. You silently congratulate yourself on dressing down as you're sure that it helped you smoothly ingratiate yourself to the group. You have seen the defensive reactions that groups like this have given to traditional salespeople who show up in dress shirts, ties and expensive suits.

As the meeting begins to wind down you hear a knock on the door. In walks Roberta, a well dressed woman who introduces herself as the Director of IT. You want to explain to Roberta that you dressed down for this group but know that would be patronizing and futile. She asks the group a few key questions and makes minimal eye contact with you. She then announces that she is going to be holding a strategy meeting with a group of VPs later that week to discuss next steps. She politely thanks you for stopping by to explain the technology and leaves.

What do you think was Roberta's impression of you? It's pretty clear that **based on first impressions alone,** she categorized you as the vendor's technical resource. She thinks of you as a peer to the other technical people in the room. You realize that there is little or no chance that you will be invited to that strategic meeting. Would it have really made a difference if you had been wearing a starched business shirt, dry-cleaned pants and a pair of shined shoes? After many years of witnessing such scenes, and as a business owner myself, I can tell you that the answer is, "YES!"

Higher level titles, with more people and tasks to manage, are even quicker to categorize others based on first impressions. These executives often lack the time or interest in getting to know a new acquaintance unless that person is directly related to or impacting strategic issues that are high priorities. These instant categorizations are based to a great extent on physical appearance, and once established are extremely difficult to change. If their first impression of you is that you are the "techy," then that is probably how you will be treated for the duration of the relationship. You never get a second chance to make a first impression.

You may be thinking, okay, but in the example with Roberta, the meeting was supposed to be with just technical people. How were you supposed to know that the Director of IT was going to show up? Exactly—you didn't know and you never do know exactly who is going to show up. If clients are serious about pursuing your services and they know that you, the vendor's SE, is on-site, there is a high probability of you seeing surprise visitors.

Evolving SEs *expect* unexpected guests.

****

Of course, you can look *too* expensive. While it is always appropriate to project success and confidence, you do not want to make others feel inferior or uncomfortable with your appearance choices. You also want to be seen as consistent with your company's culture and general philosophy.

For example, let's say that your company's marketing strategy is to be the low-cost provider. You win deals by convincing clients that they can meet their needs by not paying for the unnecessary product features that the competition oversells and overvalues. In this situation, it would be wise for you to look sharp and professional but in a more subdued way. If not, it may feel incongruent for a client to be encouraged to buy a basic solution from a sales engineer wearing an expensive suit. I think you see the problem here.

In the USA and many parts of the world, if you are calling on government accounts, discretion regarding appearance is advised as well. Often government employees believe you are overpaid. This is especially true for government software engineers who perceive themselves as having the same skill sets as you. They frequently believe that sales engineers working for successful companies are getting rich. They will read about multimillion dollar profits and assume that you are in on that action. They see themselves, on the other hand, as handcuffed to cost of living increases with no profit sharing or stock possibilities. *"Just 8 more years and I'll get my pension"* gives many government employees motivation to stay but, unfortunately, their relatively low incomes and misinformation about your income often lead to resentment.

One software salesperson that I know has been very successful selling to the United States federal government. He owns a beautiful new BMW and lives in a 3,000 square foot house. He also owns a second car. That car is a 14-year-old, beat up Ford Taurus with close to 200,000 miles on it. Although the car is old, it is clean inside and out with new seat covers and no major cosmetic issues. Its value is under $3,000. Guess which car he drives to call on his federal customers? He is also smart enough to know the importance of driving up to a US government building in an American-built car.

Every country has different standards so, if your work takes you abroad, do your homework to understand local appearance norms and expectations. The internet and your account manager are your two best resources for this information. Be careful, though, with generalizations. If, for example, you look up business dress in Italy, you will likely read that when in Italy men should wear fashionable, high quality suits and women should dress in quiet, expensive elegance. These guidelines may be accurate but before feeling obligated to invest in a new wardrobe, check with your account manager to confirm that these are true at the specific company where you will be interacting. For example, Southern Italy is more casual than Northern, so be careful not to jump to assumptions.

****

In summary, as an evolving SE, look expensive to build and reinforce the high value that you and your company deliver to the marketplace. Whenever interacting with clients, at any level, make sure that your appearance projects success and confidence. Make it easy for clients (especially executives) to categorize you as a top performer with a leadership mindset simply by the way you present yourself. Correctly shaping that perception will result in greater personal respect, higher level relationships and expanded opportunities.

Chapter 14

OPTOMIZE EMAIL AND TEXTING

The following statistics regarding email were posted on Royal.Pingdom.com, by Pingdom, a Swedish website analysis company, on January 12, 2011:

Email
1. **107 trillion** – The number of emails sent on the Internet in 2010.
2. **294 billion** – Average number of email messages per day.
3. **1.88 billion** – The number of email users worldwide.
4. **480 million** – New email users since the year before.
5. **89.1%** – The share of emails that were spam.
6. **262 billion** – The number of spam emails per day (assuming 89% are spam).
7. **2.9 billion** – The number of email accounts worldwide.
8. **25%** – Share of email accounts that are corporate.

The figure regarding spam is consistent with a study by Symantec, Inc., in 2009, which reported that unsolicited e-mail made up 90.4 percent of messages on corporate networks.

Still, email and texting are the de facto standards for business communications. While they are now the most popular communication choices, they are also frequently misused tools. Let's start with email.

Email advantages include:
- Provides an excellent record of discussion points and agreements
- Minimizes location and time zone challenges (good for global teams)
- Gives the respondent time to craft an answer compared with a live or phone conversation
- Minimizes time required for similar phone or face to face communications
- Eases the process for negotiating low priority and repeat business
- Allows parties to focus on their words, not body language or vocal tones
- Minimizes interpersonal tension
- Allows single messages to be sent to a group of people
- Allows attachments to instantly be shared (knowledge transfer)

Disadvantages include:
- Information distortion or exaggeration is more likely
- Trust and rapport are harder to build and maintain

- Less give-and-take than in face to face communications
- Can be used for political purposes (*"cover my back," "prove later that I was right,"* etc.)
- Higher likelihood of unpleasant exchanges and misunderstandings
- Loss of opportunity to quickly correct mistakes and misunderstandings
- Written statements often viewed as "binding," reducing openness and flexibility of communication
- Emotions open to receiver's interpretation

In my experience, the biggest drawback of email communication is related to the last point. An email does not provide accurate information regarding the emotional state of the sender.

Email forces the receiver to define the sender's emotion.

Without the benefit of being able to read the physical cues of the other party or to listen to his or her tone of voice, the receiver is forced to define *"What exactly did he/she mean by that?"* Even though senders are generally confident that they are clear in their message, receivers still have a high likelihood of decoding a message in a different way than intended.

Here is an example of an email that one might receive. Read it and imagine how you would react if you were the recipient.

From: SusanRT@HotWiredFibers.com
To: BobbyJS@CodeWatchers.com
Subject: Schedule problems!

Bobby – I really need to tell you that I'm not happy about your boss's idea. If we start the integration late in October, we probably won't be able to go live by Christmas. This could seriously impact your end of year business plans. Maybe he has something else in mind but this idea just doesn't strike me as a very good one.

I'd ask him if we can PLEASE stick with the original plan and start this month. I want to make sure that we have buffer time in case of any glitches. You're my most important customer this quarter and I really want to make sure that you succeed.

Please let me know today as I will be gone all next week,
Susan
Senior Sales Engineer

Was the email honest? Did it contain a reasonable position as to why the SE was unhappy with the possible schedule change? The answer is *"Yes"* to both of those questions. But there are communication mistakes that may lead to avoidable problems later on. They include:

- The subject *"Schedule problems!"* is emotionally inflammatory. It makes the SE seem panicked and irritated. This is reinforced later with the use of all caps in the word *"PLEASE."*

- Stating that the manager's idea *"does not strike me as a very good one"* is problematic. What if Bobby forwards this email to management? One of the rules of using email is that you should assume that **everyone at your company and the client's will eventually read the message.**

- An SE should not tell a customer that they are the SE's most important client. This indicates that the SE ranks customers by importance and, therefore, allocates attention and service based on where the customer stands in the SE's rankings.

- If the SE is not going to be available, the customer should be able to seamlessly obtain service from someone else in the company. The final salutation gives no indication of who to contact for help next week during the SE's absence.

- This email leaves the receiver wondering if the sender is angry, irritated or just passionate about doing a great job. Unfortunately, the recipient will have to make that call due to the many subjective words and judgments sprinkled throughout the email.

Here is an email on the same topic that will be better received:

From: SusanRT@HotWiredFibers.com
To: BobbyJS@CodeWatchers.com
Subject: Schedule proposal

Bobby:
Thank you for the email regarding your manager's new schedule proposal. Keeping me informed is very helpful and will contribute significantly to the success of our project.

In our last meeting we agreed that going live by Christmas was your #1 priority. Because of this, I would recommend that we try to stick to our schedule and begin this month. This would give us enough buffer time to deal with any unforeseen issues and comfortably meet your deadline.

If your manager has other ideas or reasons for delaying this until October please let me know. We will be as flexible as the situation requires.

If you cannot reach me today, Tammy Shinzu will be filling in for me next week as I will be out of the office. I will inform her of your situation and make sure that she has enough information to be as helpful as possible. She has worked on numerous implementations like yours and I'm sure she will be able to assist you. Here is her contact information:

TammySh@HotWiredFibers.com
408 555-8585

Thank you again for the update and your support,
Susan
Senior Sales Engineer

In this example the customer and the manager now have an objective, professional communication to share and discuss. No one could reasonably take offense to the SE's push-back regarding rescheduling the project's start date because of the logical reasoning and use of objective, calm language.

TEXTING

Texting shares just about every advantage and disadvantage of email yet it has a very different "feel" to it for the other party. Texting feels like a conversation vs. exchanging formal communications. It is casual and efficient. It has a sense of immediacy only matched by a live conversation. It is also likely to erode email market share as the next, younger generation of workers gravitates to texting before emailing.

What text senders tend to forget is that you still lose the impact of nonverbal behaviors and vocal tone when sending a text. Because it feels so conversational it is easy to fall into the trap of believing that the receiver is accurately interpreting your emotions, as will be discussed in detail later in this chapter.

Here is an example of an SE texting in the hopes of saving time:

Texting Madness

SE:
Can I call u.

Client:
Y?

SE:
Steve's out.

Client:
So?

SE:
R u in?

Client:
Home office/not 4 long.

SE:
Busy now. Can call later.

Client:
U call or I call? Why?

SE:
Why what?

While this may be an exaggeration, similar text-based conversations occur with alarming frequency. Texting such short responses may be easy but both parties are sure to be frustrated, time is being wasted and general impressions regarding the communication skills of the SE are at risk.

Even when texting succeeds, as an SE it is still important to send an email to follow up on a text message, when:

- The communication is lengthy and hard to read on a smart phone
- The other party uses email as their first choice for contacting you
- Copying others on the message is desirable
- The subject changes and you'll need to be able to quickly reference and understand earlier communications

Choosing your medium

Why is communication so tricky when the face to face or nonverbal components are eliminated, as in an email or texting? The answer can be found in many studies that I have seen over the years measuring this phenomenon. One study by Ph.D.Albert Mehrabian, sited in his book, (1) Silent Messages, concluded that the impact of the three human communication components on the recipient are as follows[1]:

Words – 7%
Vocal tone – 38%
Nonverbal – 55%

At first, these percentages may seem hard to believe. But when you think about it, it's very true that we judge others based mainly on nonverbal behaviors. For example, if you ask Joe, a client, if he can complete a project on time, his immediate nonverbal reaction will be an excellent indicator of his confidence in meeting the deadline. The words and vocal tones that follow will merely confirm or conflict with the messages that Joe might have already sent nonverbally.

According to Dr. Mehrabian, 55% of how Joe really feels about completing the project on time is revealed by his nonverbal reaction. All this data is available to the observant SE before a single word has been spoken. It's important for you to be aware of how significant this immediate reaction is when assessing the sincerity of the other's response. Perhaps when you ask Joe about his comfort level with the deadline he quickly looks away or heavily sighs. These are signs that should be observed and probed. In this case, in order to gain as accurate a picture as possible regarding Joe's true feelings, it would be useful for the SE to follow up with a question such as, "I get the feeling that you're not very comfortable with the deadline – what are your thoughts?"

Here ar some additional nonverbal indicators along with the reactions that convey confidence or uncertainty:

Nonverbal Indicators	Confidence	Uncertainty
Eye Contact	Maintains contact while speaking and listening	Looking down, darting around
Mouth	Natural/relaxed position, still when not speaking, comfortable smile	Clenching teeth, licking lips, smiling nervously
Legs	Still, kept in same position	Shaking, twitching, moving for no reason
Hands	Still, only used to gesture in ways that support content	Rubbing hands, playing with rings, touching hair, gesturing too much
Breathing	Normal rate, steady, unperceivable	Sighing, breathing rapidly
Body Movement (when standing)	Smooth, relaxed, only used to emphasize key points	Pacing back and forth, rocking, not moving at all

Reading nonverbal responses is actually pretty easy, even cross culturally. This is because, despite our differences, cultures share many common bonds regarding the interpretation of the nonverbal. Constant hand wringing or excessive pacing is a sign of nervousness in Dallas, Tokyo, Shanghai, San Paulo and Munich. There are, of course, some exceptions. For example, in many parts of India, shaking one's head back and forth indicates a positive reaction, where in most of the world this appears to be a "*No*" reaction. In Japan, prolonged eye contact would be less welcomed than in the US. Also, second language issues make encoding and decoding messages problematic and frequently lead to misinterpretations or unnecessary email loops to clarify exact meanings.

However, because nonverbal responses are driven as much by human nature as cultural training, evolving SEs pay special attention to these reactions in all settings. Hopefully, now that you realize that 55% of the receiver's reaction is based on decoding the sender's nonverbal behaviors, you too will raise your sensitivity to this component and become more aware of the messages that you are nonverbally sending.

This discussion leads to an important question. How does an SE decide when email/texting is an appropriate communication vehicle compared with picking up the phone or seeking a face to face meeting? The answer is to analyze and recognize **the subjectivity of the message.**

Before sending an email, analyze the subjectivity level of the email's content. If, for example, the message is, *"The meeting will start at 9:00am, PST, on Monday June 9th"* there is no subjectivity involved. No subjectivity equates to a low potential for misinterpretation, which means it's appropriate to email the message. Many of your communications will fall into this category.

Here are a few examples of effective email communications based on the low subjectivity level of the message:
"I will be there tomorrow at noon."
"The software requires 512K of storage."
"All other programs must be closed in order to run the demonstration."

On the other hand, many of your communications are subjective and therefore should not be emailed. They may seem objective to you, but on closer examination you may find that, while the other party may understand what you are saying, your feelings and attitudes behind the message may be more open to interpretation than desired.

Here are statements that are likely to be misinterpreted in an email:

"I really need your help on this one."
"I just don't get it."
"Come on, everybody. This isn't that difficult."
"Your boss sounds like my boss."
"At this point, I'm at a loss what to try next."
"Is that really the best you can do?"
"Why can't your department do it?"
"I need to take care of someone else right now."

Based on Dr. Mehrabian's study, if at all possible then, an SE would pick up the phone or visit a client whenever needing to deliver a relatively subjective message. This, of course, is impractical for a number of reasons, including the geographic distribution of customers and their communication preference.

When you need to email a subjective message, here are four helpful guidelines:

- **Support your message with data.**
  Even in a subjective message, data points will help clarify intentions. For example, *"Sandy, I really need your help in completing this project. The report is due on March 28th at 9am and we have only finished two of the three required tests."*

- **Show your email to someone else before sending.**
A second opinion will usually provide you with valuable feedback. Ask someone you trust to share their reactions to the email in terms of content clarity and emotional impact.

- **Insert the recipient's email address last.**
This technique will encourage you to read what you have written one last time before sending. This also prevents accidentally sending the email before completing your message. This is a particularly important guideline if your laptop has keys close together that can accidentally be touched, activating the *Send* function.

- **Shorten for higher level communications**
Managers and above, with less technical expertise, are prone to skim or even skip emails from SEs. The rule of thumb for higher levels is that the executive should be able to read the entire email, including your signature, without scrolling down on a Blackberry or iPhone.

Voicemail

While we're on the topic of communication choices, I think it's important to say a few words about a diminishing choice – voicemail.

I was recently in Cupertino teaching our *Consultative Essentials* program. One of the participants stated that they rarely check their voicemail unless their inbox is full. *"Really?"* I asked? *"You wait until it's full?"* Expecting the person to back down, instead he calmly reasserted himself and told me that he can't remember the last time that he checked a voicemail. His approach was to look who called and, if the call seemed important, he would call them back. He considered voicemail a waste of time.

I then redirected the question to the others in the class. We had 19 people that day. Guess how many agreed with his approach? All 19!

This group was relatively young at a very leading edge company which might explain group sentiment. But the more I travel and listen, the more I hear others share the same disinterest in voicemail. So, based on the subjective value of the message as discussed earlier, what is one to do if the message justifies a call but people are checking voicemail so much less?

First, confirm how much your client does use the phone and voicemail. In many companies, and especially government, the phone is still the best choice. If the client is more focused on emailing or texting, understand that they will see your message first. Go ahead and leave the voicemail so they can hear your feelings about the message and then wait a few hours to send the email. Let them know in the voicemail that you will be sending an email follow up. This approach gives you the best of both worlds. They will hear your feelings and have a written record for later study and comment.

RELATIONSHIPS MATTER

The longer you work with someone the less you will have to be concerned with your medium choice. Humans are quite visual and auditory in thinking. Once we know someone we actually "see and hear" his/her voice in our head while we are reading their message. We create a real time picture in our minds of the person delivering the message and become increasingly better at interpreting intent. Even though message subjectivity should still be considered, established relationships minimize the need for such frequent analyses of whether or not to email or text the message.

****

In summary, email and texting are the de facto standards for business communications today and will be into the foreseeable future. They are wonderfully productive tools when used properly. If possible, avoid using email if your message is highly subjective and may be open to multiple interpretations. In these situations, choose your words carefully, or, ideally, pick up the phone or meet in person. If you still need to use email, follow the guidelines provided to maximize clarity and goodwill.

(1) December, 1990, second edition, published by Wadsworth, pages 75-80.

Chapter 15

PLANNING WHAT NOT TO SHARE

Have you ever revealed information to a client and immediately wished that you could take it back? In fact, you were probably in mid-sentence when you realized that it was a mistake but, oh well, too late! Besides, how much harm could it really do?

Why do we say things that later we so clearly realize should have been held back? Some reasons might include:

- Wanting to improve relationships and believing that revealing semi-confidential or disempowering information will help achieve this goal
- Not realizing the downsides of revealing certain information
- Getting excited about a topic and wanting to share more about it without considering the potential consequences
- Being uncomfortable with tension and believing that certain disclosures will reduce the tension level

- Not planning before the meeting regarding information to avoid discussing

In our experience at Technically Speaking, the last point is probably the most common. Generally, solo and joint planning focuses on what information the SE and AM want to get from the client. Because there is so much to learn, it is easy to be totally focused on the "get" side of the equation. In this chapter we will explore the "give" side of the equation, including what not to say during client meetings.

Here is a section of a typical planning template that an SE might use to prepare for an upcoming meeting. This might be completed alone or with an AM.

Client:_____

Individual:_____ Title:_____

What are our goals for the meeting and what questions will we ask to achieve those goals?

Goals	Questions
1.	
2.	
3.	

For this application, what are our most compelling product advantages and weaknesses?

Sweet Spots	Drawbacks

What might the other party *specifically* ask us to concede and why?

Items Asked For	Why Are They Asking for the Concession?

Each of these areas is worth analyzing and most sales teams do a good job of preparing. However, what is often absent from the planning process is a discussion regarding what information to **withhold** and, if probed by the client in one of those areas, how to respond in a manner that is truthful and acceptable to the other party yet does not reveal information that might negatively impact the sales team's power.

Non-disclosure planning is important for solo and joint calls. It will minimize costly slip ups that unnecessarily reveal company, personal or product weaknesses. In addition, when on joint calls with team members, it will ensure that you and your partner are in alignment regarding what not to share, allowing both parties to feel more confident and relaxed during the interaction. Evolving SEs want their AMs to know that they can be trusted to conduct discovery work and engage in productive conversations without sharing counter-productive information.

This share/no share discussion is often missing from the joint call planning phase because:

- Assumptions are made that team members are in agreement regarding what to avoid bringing up in front of the client
- There is no history of a team member saying something that the other team member found unacceptable
- No one on the team has ever thought about this concept
- Team members feel like they will be offending or patronizing his/her partner by initiating this discussion

In our training classes, we like to ask participants the following:

"Have you ever been in a customer meeting when someone from your team said something that made you just want to kick them under the table?"

We then hear stories about elbow nudging, throat clearing and actual physical contact. One AM told us about an SE who was giving a presentation when the SE started talking about features that he *wished* their product possessed. In a panic, the AM threw a dry erase pen at the

231

SE while saying, *"Hey, why don't you draw that diagram that explains how our application works."* The startled SE caught the pen and started drawing. The AM later apologized and then explained to the SE why he felt compelled to launch a projectile in his direction!

Below is an example of a simple addition to a planning form that we recommend for solo and joint calls.

INFORMATION DISCOVERY/SHARING

Information *we want* to get:

1. *Reasons for exploring enterprise changes*
2. *Personal needs of the other party*
3. *Decision process*
4. *Competition*
5. *Budget*
6. *Urgency*
7. *Their image of us*

Information *we do not want to give:*

1. *Only two references for security product*
2. *My newness to the company*
3. *Concessions or special deals given to others*
4. *Bugs in latest version (not on features they are interested in)*
5. *Competitors*

If asked about information *we do not want to give*, how will we respond?

1. *"We do have references in your industry. As we get closer to working together I would recommend you speak with them."*

2. *"In terms of my background, I've worked in the enterprise storage space for close to 10 years."*

3. *"Our company policy prohibits me from mentioning other deals. Once I complete my technical evaluation I'll turn this over to my account manager and you will work with her directly on the proposal (note-do not say that you're sure that she will give you a good deal!)."*

4. *"Our latest version has been successfully installed in the field. All the features that you've selected are working fine."*

5. *"We don't usually discuss the competition. What we've heard though is that we have significant advantages in three main areas. They are..."*

THE HONESTY DILEMMA

"But if we don't tell them that, aren't we being dishonest?"
Frustrated SE

This may be one of the most controversial and challenging areas of team selling. We often hear examples in our workshops of SEs who feel that they should be telling clients more than their AMs are willing to allow. In these situations, SEs may feel like "accessories to the crime" by allowing sales to proceed without mentioning information that they believe the customer should know. This creates a true dilemma for SEs who believe that team decisions should be based on how those decisions impact long term client relationships vs. short term revenue goals.

So, what should you do when your AM asks you to not share specific information that you believe is vital to disclose?

If you truly believe that withholding information or misrepresenting your products or services in any way might cause material harm to the client, then you have a responsibility to proactively address the situation. First, share your concerns directly with your AM. Find out exactly why he/she wants to hold back this information. Your AM may have a valid and acceptable reason that has not occurred to you yet. Because AMs, not SEs, own the accounts, they have to be given a chance to explain their thinking.

Next, if you cannot reach an acceptable agreement then you may be faced with the uncomfortable need to involve management. Your direct manager should be your next point of contact to discuss the matter. No doubt, he or she will feel a sense of responsibility to address the situation and minimize potential repercussions. Your manager is likely to escalate the discussion to the AM's manager or further up the SE ladder. Remember, just because an AM asks you to follow a certain course of action does not mean that you have no other options or lack culpability. Evolving SEs will always take action to protect themselves and their clients, even if it means involving managers or upsetting AMs.

If you feel the item under discussion is quite serious, I'd recommend you summarize your points in an email to your manager and save a copy for your records. There's nothing wrong with protecting yourself against a backlash should the situation become even more volatile. Plus, what if your manager or the AM leave the company and there's no one to back up your claims?

The challenge for SEs is to know where to draw the line. What constitutes good sales strategy vs. deceitful selling? One guideline to help you answer this is to ask yourself the following:

"Would I categorize this information as 'need to know' or 'nice to know'?"

SEs often will too quickly decide that the information under discussion should be categorized as need to know. Upon closer examination, this frequently is not the case. These situations are analogous to those we encounter in technical presentation skills workshops. SEs will show us their slide decks consisting of what they believe their clients need to know. By the time we finish analyzing their slides, based on the target audience and presentation goals, many of the slides clearly should be categorized as nice to know. So, before you push back on your AM regarding information that he or she has decided to conceal, first carefully consider if the information is need to know or nice to know.

FUTURE PRODUCTS
One area SEs need to consider is how and when to mention future products. Should you tell the customer what your company is working on even if it is not available today?

Pretend for a moment that you are the AM. You have weekly revenue calls to tell your manager what you

235

are working on and what you will be closing this week. If you are not on target to meet your goals, your manager will insist on you explaining why you are having problems and what you are going to do to fix it. Also, as an AM you understand that your success is tied to your manager's success. If you miss your number, so does he/she. You are under constant pressure to make your numbers.

Given this reality as an AM, how would you feel about an SE mentioning a future, currently unavailable product to a customer? Exactly! As an AM you strongly believe that SEs are there to help you reach your numbers today. Yes, long-term relationships are important. Yes, we want to be strategic. But as an AM you still have to make your numbers this week and the SE's #1 job is to help you get there.

Therefore, while in principle I'm recommending that you do not mention future products, there are two situations when it is recommended. They are:
1. When the customer needs a roadmap
2. As a stalling tactic

When the customer needs a roadmap
The more complex your technology the more a customer is likely to need assurance regarding future direction. Once they are comfortable with where your technology is going they will be comfortable with longer term commitments.

If the buy is a short-term, problem fix they may not care about your company's vision. But short-term fixes alone do not provide fertile grounds for real growth and company survival. If you are going to help drive IT direction vs. react to it, roadmapping is likely a high priority to your clients and future direction should be shared. You still need to maintain awareness of when you're drifting into "nice to know" tangents, but, overall, a clear vision of your company's strategy will often be the key to moving to next steps.

AS A STALLING TACTIC

Let's say you're about to lose a deal because the competition has something that you don't. It's a deal killer. If you can't address this item you will not get the business.

Your options now are limited. First, of course, confirm that you truly understand the business problem and have exhausted all other options. Assuming you've unsuccessfully tried to address the issue it may be time to slow things down.

Your next move is internally-focused. Go to the experts and share the situation. Ask if your company is working on anything similar and, if so, what a timeline looks like for development. Make sure that the information is dependable as your reputation with the client may hinge on how this is handled.

If your company is working on the same function or one similar to the one that the competition now offers, go back to your client and share the news. Frame it in a way that exposes your virtues on other key decision making criteria and see if you can buy a little more time.

SE:
"Tony, I know that customizing the report function on the executive dashboard is very important to you, right?"

Client:
"That's right. In fact, if you can't provide that feature then we're going to have to go with someone else."

SE:
"Can I just ask, if it wasn't for that one function, how would you feel about going with us?"

Client:
"You would win. You have everything else that we need, in particular the international support, but without that feature you simply won't get the business."

SE:
"I hope I have some good news for you then. My Product people have confirmed that the next release will include that feature. Just to be clear, this should come out in 90 days but I can't commit to a definite date. However, if you can give us just a little more time I can give you updates regarding its progress."

Client:
"Hmmm. I might be able to wait a little longer but my boss is not going to want to feel like you're dragging this out."

SE:
"Absolutely. In fact, I've received approval to set up a meeting between you, your boss and my Product people to talk about our progress, if that would help."

Client:
"Excellent. Let's do that and see when we can realistically expect this to happen."

✳✳

In summary, in addition to planning what information to *get* from clients, plan what information you and your AM should not *give*. Understand that it is possible to be an honest, high integrity SE without revealing every piece of information at your disposal. This simple planning step will minimize innocent, yet potentially harmful disclosures, while helping to avoid unnecessary discussions that could erode your team's power.

Chapter 16

SEE A PROBLEM, PROBE IT

"*See a problem, probe it*" is an essential technique for maintaining poise and control during challenging client and internal interactions. It is a skill that clearly separates evolving SEs from the rest. It is also a technique that is counter-intuitive to how most SEs naturally respond when these events occur.

Historically, SEs have been trained to "*See a problem, fix it.*" And why not? SEs are usually invited to meet with a client for the same reason that their account managers get a call in the first place—the client has a problem. The problem is usually that something is broken, not working as well as it should or not producing at an acceptable level of quantity or quality. In sales jargon these are referred to as "pain points," "challenges," and "unrealized opportunities," but the bottom line is that clients have *problems* that they believe your company has the potential to fix.

It would only make sense then that your goal is to solve the problem as quickly as possible. If you immediately understand the problem and have a solution that you believe is a direct match, then why bother investing time and resources to prolong the conversation? A quick, accurate solution is best for the customer and you, right? Maybe not, and I'll use a story to help illustrate the point.

****

The Estimates

Let's say that you buy a 90-year-old house that is mainly made of wood. It has lots of character and overall is in good condition. Unfortunately, the back wall of the house needs to be painted so you decide to call in two painters to get bids.

The first painter, Steve, looks at the wall and says, "You definitely need priming and two coats of paint. Let me show you your choices and I'll give you a price." Steve seems competent and has excellent references so you are feeling pretty good about getting him started on the job, assuming the price is fair. You even think about canceling the second appointment because you feel so good about Steve.

Later that day the second painter, Angie, shows up. You show her the wall and she asks if it's okay to get out her ladder to take a closer look. You don't see any need for this as it's obviously just a wall that needs painting, but you agree. In fact, you feel a little impatient as you don't really want to devote too much time to this.

Angie inspects the wall and comes down off the ladder. She explains to you that you have significant dry rot issues. She goes back up the ladder and shows you numerous places where she can press her finger into the wood. She tells you that you could just paint over the damaged parts but the dry

---

rot would need to be addressed within the next year or two to prevent real structural issues. By fixing the dry rot now, many of the planks could be saved and it would cost far less than waiting until the situation worsens. She then gives you two prices—one for priming and painting, and the other for replacing the dry rot as well.

****

Maybe you decide to go for the full fix as recommended by Angie, or maybe not. Either way, as a customer you are going to feel like Angie was the one who made it possible for you to make a fully informed decision. The next time you have a similar situation, you will call Angie. When your neighbor asks for a referral, you will probably mention Angie as a real expert and even a "trusted advisor" for this kind of work.

SEs who immediately jump to solutions when they hear problems are behaving like our first painter, Steve. Evolving SEs, who listen, observe, probe and create options are reacting to situations more like Angie.

Instead of *"See a problem, fix it,"* the mantra for evolving SEs is...

See a problem, PROBE it.

You have many opportunities to apply this approach. They include when you are:

- **Initially told by a third party (your manager, the AM, etc.) what the customer is looking to accomplish**

You can take the information at face value, assume its accuracy and only focus on what you have been told, or leverage the initial data and probe the client for confirmation of their goals and other areas of opportunity.

- **Asked if your product/service can do something specific**

Here you have the choice between maintaining a narrow conversation focus or expanding the discussion to fully understand the bigger picture.

- **Given a challenging objection during a presentation**

A common reaction here is to immediately counter the objection with a technical explanation. Instead, probe to fully understand the objection before answering. This will often uncover important information that will significantly affect how you respond. In addition, often the initial objection does not reveal the real underlying concern or issue. Additional probing in these situations can lead to more on-target and satisfying responses for clients.

- **Told by a team member to do something with no reasonable justification provided**

Instead of blindly following team member requests or arguing over directives, make your first reaction one of curiosity. Make it clear that you have a sincere interest in first understanding their position before offering yours.

Let's take the last two bullet items (one external, one internal) to illustrate our point. The conversation examples that follow contrast the *"See a problem, fix it"* approach with the *"See a problem, probe it"* technique.

Given a challenging objection during a presentation

"I can see how your platform would help speed up our processes but that's not really all that important."

See a problem, fix it

SE:

"I know you say that's not important now but I think you'd really enjoy the benefits of our speed. When you speed up this part of your operation all sorts of good things can happen. For example, when the information goes to marketing they'll be able to immediately reroute that data to the field. This can really help when your sales team is trying to convince a customer that you have access to this kind of information.

In fact, this speed advantage is why most customers buy this version. I have one customer I can tell you about who loves the speed. Here's what happened. They were running version 3.4 when we sold them 4.2. Since then..."

See a problem, probe it

SE:

"I see. If speeding up your processes is not a high priority, what are your highest priorities and how would you like to see our platform impact those areas."

✳✳✳

Told by a team member to do something with no reasonable justification offered

AM:

"Let's not talk to the customer about some of the problems we're having with the security product."

See a problem, fix it

SE:

"No. I'm not comfortable holding back that information. What happens if someone steals data off their system? Do you realize how many identity thefts occur every year? I know you want to make this sale but I cannot go along with hiding such important information. If you insist on this approach I will have to go to my manager and I definitely will be asked to be taken off this account."

See a problem, probe it

SE:

"I have to tell you that I'm concerned about not mentioning some of the security product issues but I'm sure you have your reasons. Can you tell me a little more about your decision so that I can feel better about this approach?

AM:

This particular application will not involve sensitive data. I've checked this with the client and they've assured me that the usual security concerns are not relevant for this installation. If they want to use us for other applications we definitely will let them know about some of the problems we're experiencing. Does that help?"

SE:

"I see. I had no idea that the application is not security sensitive. I won't volunteer the security issues unless they do show interest in using us for other applications. In that case, I think we should mention it. What do you think?"

AM:

"I agree. Let's see where the conversation goes but I think we're on the same page."

****

In summary, by initially *probing* a problem rather than *fixing* it, you are performing at a more consultative and thoughtful level. You will be more influential, credible and respected when you seek to fully understand a situation before recommending next steps. The client and your company benefit significantly from this highly collaborative approach—the client will be educated on all available options and you will be maximizing the potential scope of your company's relationship with them. In the next chapter you will learn a technique for sequencing your recommendations in a format designed to further enhance your image and increase the customer's sense of urgency to take action.

Chapter 17

CREATE A GAP

The longer you can go without mentioning a product,
the greater your chances are of selling it.

My wife and I rent a lot of movies. Sometimes when we are a little pressed for time, we will fast forward the movie just to see how it ends. It might have a great ending but without the build up and intrigue that the body of the movie offers, the WOW factor is gone and the entertainment experience feels rather mundane. It's similar to skipping the middle of a book and just reading the last chapter. Our reaction to how a story ends is really dependant on the journey the author took us on to get there.

As an evolving SE, when recommending solutions, you are telling a story. Your ability to build interest and curiosity by effectively sequencing the chapters of your story is a key factor in the overall persuasiveness and impact of your final message. This chapter will teach you a proven structure for telling your story. You will find the recommended approach to be extremely applicable to SE presentation opportunities.

Let's say, for example, that an SE and AM are ready to make recommendations to a client regarding proposed products and services. A mix of technical and non-technical people will be in attendance. After the initial warmup and introductions, here is what we might typically hear from the SE:

"Thanks again for inviting us in to present our ideas. Based on what we've learned, we're ready to recommend a package that we think will fully meet your needs. Here is our agenda for today's presentation."

Agenda

- **Unitec**
- **B500 Software Version 3.6**
- **Installation**
- **Training**
- **Support Level Options**
- **Q&A**

"I'll start off by telling you about our company and then describing the B500 Software package, version 3.6, and what makes it such a great solution. Next I'll talk about our installation process.

You've also mentioned that you want many of your team members to be trained on the product. I will show you the training approach and schedule that we feel will best meet that need. Finally, you need to feel comfortable that we will be there to support you well into the future. I will review our support policy, purchase options, and then I'll open the floor up for your questions. Okay, are we ready to go?"

How do you like what you just read? It sounds pretty good, doesn't it?
- *The agenda was clear*
- *All important topics seem to be covered*

Unfortunately, this presentation appears to focus on the SEs favorite topic – the SEs' products and processes. It is not effective if the SE wants to be perceived as truly understanding the client's business drivers and buying criteria. In order to accomplish this and to fully engage audience members, a different agenda is required.

Consider the following revised agenda and the introduction that follows:

Agenda

- **Current Situation Summary**
- **Desired Situation Review**
- **Recommended Solutions**
- **Next Steps**

"Thank you for inviting us in today. Here is our agenda. First, we'd like to confirm that we've accurately heard and understood your business and technical needs. In order to do that, I'm going to start by quickly summarizing your current environment.

Next, based on our discovery work with you, I'll review where you want your system to be as a result of our partnership. We've received a number of requests from your technical staff and lines of businesses regarding product applications and their effects on internal processes and market image.

Once we've confirmed where you are and where you want to be I will walk you through the recommended solutions to bridge that gap. I will divide those by lines of business as the goals vary quite a bit between each. I will also summarize how we'll address other activities, such as training and support services, followed by recommended next steps.

Today's presentation should take about one hour. If you have any questions along the way, please don't hesitate to interrupt me as I want to make sure that everyone is comfortable with the proposed solution and our understanding of your business. Okay, are we ready to go?"

The revised agenda, summarized in the opening statement, is referred to as the *gap-creation* approach. You are creating gaps in the minds of your customers of where they are today compared to where they need to be in the future. When clients see this gap, succinctly and accurately defined, it crystallizes for them the need for change and even creates a certain amount of tension and discomfort. This reaction will often manifest itself as an increased sense of urgency to take action.

The information in the *Current* and *Desired* presentation slides must be void of opinions and judgments. They should only contain **objective** data obtained directly from interviews conducted during the discovery phase and needs analysis. They should not contain opinions or conclusions. You are simply reiterating what you have been told by the client to confirm your understanding of their business.

Here are unacceptable and acceptable bullet points for *Current* and *Desired* slides:

Uncacceptable	Acceptable
The market is responding well to your new version	Sales are up 3.5%
Your clients are not happy with customer service	Customer satisfaction ratings dropped two points this year
Your team isn't ready to support our product	Only one of your people is a JAVA expert
Your website is difficult to navigate	Users must now go through a minimum of six pages to place an order

your statements objective **minimizes** or **eliminates objections**. This is consistent with the traditional sales school philosophy of building positive momentum early in the sales cycle by sticking with questions to which customers are only likely to answer *"Yes."* By introducing subjective statements early on, detractors may seize the opportunity to pose difficult objections or derail your presentation. By keeping it objective you take away this opportunity. How can a client reasonably object to data that they provided to you? An easy way to remember this is:

Being objective eliminates objections.

How do customers feel when you begin by summarizing what you know about their business?

They feel like you have:
- Invested valuable time to get to know their business and its goals
- Earned the right to propose solutions and have those solutions respected
- Taken an interest beyond technology, into more strategic considerations, such as the impact of technology decisions on the company's client base.

By summarizing what you have learned *first*, you will find you have a much more attentive and engaged audience. Instead of fast forwarding to the end of the movie, you are building your story, setting up a much more impactful and persuasive ending.

Notice that when using this approach the SE will be well into the presentation before mentioning any specific technology. In fact, none of the revised agenda items even mention technology. In contrast, the original agenda's first item was the B500 software. How does this evolved approach compare with the way you currently present? Deferring the technology discussion is one of the keys to turning a technical presentation into a consultative interaction.

One key when using this approach is, as mentioned earlier, to be succinct. You should move through the *Current* and *Desired* slides briskly. Avoid lengthy explanations.

There is no need to elaborate on these. Your goal is simply to gain agreement that you have accurately defined these areas while building buy-in for later when you present your solutions. It's impossible to give an exact ratio, but, as a guideline, if you are giving a one-hour presentation, plan on spending about 10 minutes on the *Current* and *Desired* slides.

You will also win new allies with this *gap-creation* structure. Perhaps some attendees are on the fence regarding their opinion of you. Even when you are well into the sales cycle, you may have people in the room you have never met, requiring you to build a favorable first impression. Remember that evolving SEs *expect* someone unexpected to drop by (see Chapter 13, "Look Expensive"). If, for example, the CIO or a Line of Business Executive surprisingly joins the group, this format will align well with how they prefer to assimilate data.

This approach is also useful in helping plan what information to gather before giving a presentation. Here a brief story from my company on the ease of using this approach and the ensuing benefits.

No Time to Prep!

One of my consultants and I were conducting concurrent training sessions for a pharmaceutical company on the topic of consultative selling skills. During the morning break, one of our client's training managers told us that they were shopping for a presentation skills class for the sales team and were wondering if we had any information with us on ours. He told us that their Director of

---

Training, Anne, was in town that day and would be interested in looking over our approach and even speaking with us.

What were our options? We could have:
1. Handed Anne a brochure and described the program in broad terms.
2. Printed out the entire workbook from my laptop and given her a detailed walk through of the content.
3. Treated this as a discovery meeting and focused on asking her questions.
4. Leveraged our knowledge of her company and created a brief presentation using the gap-creation method.

Our first choice would have been #3. However, our contact told us that she really wanted product information today. Because we are always sensitive to meeting customer expectations, we decided to use #4, with some discovery discussion included. The gap-creation option was available because my consultant and I both had significant experience with the company and felt that we had a good sense of the current presentation skills level of the sales team and where opportunities for improvement existed.

We asked our contact if we could meet with Anne during the last 15 minutes of the lunch hour. We huddled at noon to begin our work. Fortunately, some of the comments from the manager who had kicked off the session that morning had given us updated insight into the team's current and desired states. This proved to be very useful as we prepared our presentation.

It took us less than 30 minutes to complete a professional slide show for Anne. We came up with enough Current and Desired slides to feel confident going into the meeting.

At 12:45 we met with Anne. We began with a few open-ended questions that went well, although we sensed her desire to get to our presentation. The presentation thoroughly impressed her. She knew that we had no advanced warning and had created our slideshow within the last hour. She was expecting a quick product pitch but what she got was a consultative presentation that accurately depicted our knowledge of her company and its goals. When she told us that, "Your observations about our current and desired states are right on," we knew that the gap-creation technique had worked again.

We have worked with Anne's company for many years now and have been referred to others as a result. The first impression created by the structure of our slide show was surely the turning point that led to such outstanding results.

I'm sure you can see the value of beginning a presentation by summarizing current and desired situations. But what if the audience disagrees with one of your observations? What if your current technology description is no longer valid or organizational goals have shifted and desired conditions have changed? First, if you have done your homework, any recent changes to current or desired situations should be minimal. But, if changes have occurred, you certainly want to hear about these changes before describing specific solutions. In fact, the potential for pushback on the current and desired slides reinforces the case for using them. Armed with new data, you will be able to make minor adjustments later in your presentation that, without this approach, would be impossible.

Example:

"You told me during the desired situation slide that you no longer need to get data to the field sales team. In that case, let me white board for you how we would change our recommendation from what you see on my prepared slide."

****

In summary, the *gap-creation* method moves a presentation from the predictable and technical to being consultative and strategic. When you begin by reviewing the client's current and desired situations you are building personal credibility and increasing the client's sense of urgency to take action. It is a format that you will find applicable to numerous presentation opportunities and one that can be constructed with a minimal amount of preparation time.

Chapter 18

MAKE YOU, NOT YOUR SLIDES, THE STAR OF THE SHOW

The quality of SE presentations, even within the same company, varies across an alarmingly wide spectrum. Less variation usually indicates the degree to which SE management understands and reinforces proper presentation techniques as they relate to slide creation, sequencing and general SE platform skills. The *gap-creation* method from the last chapter is a good example of a technique that could be a de facto standard for presentations. When management consistently reinforces their expectations as to how a presentation should look and feel, SEs will work harder to meet those expectations and the quality of all team member presentations will be enhanced.

One common observation of ours is in regards to how SEs interact with their slide shows. They are frequently guilty of presenting in a manner that results in the slides, not the SE, being the focus of the audience's attention. The SE's main contributions appear to be reading the slides, advancing them, and answering questions at the end of the presentation. This chapter will show you how to make *you*, not the slides, the star of the show.

Reasons to keep the main attention focused on you include:

- Presentations are great opportunities to shape the client's perception and image of you as an evolved SE.
- You can never be sure who will be in attendance that you would like to impress, and reading a slide show is *not* impressive.
- Ideas that come directly from you, as compared to what is in your slide deck, lead to a more engaging presentation experience for everyone.
- You appear more open to a dialogue and audience feedback when you are not reading a presentation.
- If the client perceives that your presence adds little additional value, they may request that future presentations simply be emailed rather than given live, or not attend, anticipating that reading your presentation later will suffice.
- By relying on your personal value rather than slides you are far more likely to compliment the slides with valuable tangents, sub-points and interesting examples.

We have all attended presentations where the SE was clearly prepared. He or she had numerous slides showing what technologies were being recommended and an abundant number of bullets points explaining exactly how the SE came to these conclusions. Included were the client's name and company examples in a finely tailored presentation that obviously required a significant invest-ment of time on the part of the SE.

In fact, there was so much good information on the slides that 80% of the time the SE just read the bullet points. This resulted in the audience shifting into the same passive mode as someone watching television. They were informed, yet the SE's *physical* presence added almost no additional value.

Presentation software, such as PowerPoint and Keynote, have elevated the technical quality of presenta-tions for most SEs worldwide. But improvements in tech-nology do not necessarily translate into better, more persuasive presentations. In fact, the opposite is often the result. We have heard complaints in many companies about *death by PowerPoint* and other unflattering refer-ences to the over-reliance on presentation technology.

There have been a number of recent articles about the downsides of presentation software. One major short-coming of these products is in their design. Their struc-ture forces the presenter to organize and present data in outline form. Long lists of bullet points end up stifling rather than encouraging creativity in presenters and audience members. In February, 2003, Jack Schofield of the *UK Guardian Unlimited* published an editorial on the topic. Regarding presentation software, he stated that,

...they are entirely left-brain tools and, while they may offer an illusion of rationality and control, what they largely do is prevent us from thinking.

In addition, because workers are now so inundated with slide shows, the SE who can minimize the amount of computer-generated information will be seen as a refreshing break from the norm. You may even find presentation scenarios where slides are not needed at all to convey your message. Recognize and seize these opportunities.

One of our training products is a class titled *"Interviewing Skills for Non-HR Professionals."* The workshop gives non-HR personnel tips on how to succeed in today's team interviewing environment. We decided to run an experiment and teach a series of these sessions with no presentation software. The classes were run at Google, obviously a very technical company. We used only flipcharts and whiteboards. After many sessions, the feedback was extremely positive. In the evaluations we asked participants to list what three ideas or items they liked best about the class. Almost without exception, *not* using a computer to present was included as one of the three.

The ease of using presentation software has led to its misuse as well. Most SEs are given slide decks that they simply load up before a presentation. By just changing a few words and inserting the client's name they can give an acceptable performance. Unfortunately, it's pretty obvious to the client that a template has simply been completed. So, while required preparation time has been minimized (a benefit) the depth of the presentations and the amount of time SEs really devote to thinking about their target audience is also minimized (a consequence).

Imagine, for example, you are asked to present your product to a company that insists on all presentations being done without the use of computers or pre-printed materials. Instead, they want you to stand in the front of the room and simply tell them why your product is so great and how it will impact their business. Using white boards or flipcharts is acceptable.

You would spend far more time preparing for this client. You would have to really think through the process of communicating each of your ideas to the client using only the spoken word and drawn diagrams on the available visual aids. The presentation would likely to be far more interactive with the lights up, while you build your story live, compared to simply transitioning from slide to slide in a darkened room. As a result, the presentation would be much more engaging and leave the client with a highly consultative perception of you.

One of our students, Dan, told us that the best presentation he ever gave was when his laptop died! Without any quick fix or available technology options he had to simply talk to the group. He shared that this experience built tremendous credibility with the client because it proved that he knew his product well enough to continue on his own. Dan also felt that the live aspect of the presentation made it much more interesting for the group and led to a far livelier interaction than they would have experienced with his usual slide show.

Sometimes, however, slides are expected and desirable. Examples of this are when your presentation contains:
- Elaborate diagrams
- Numerous statistics or data points

- *Current* and *Desired* slides (gap-building)
- "Build" slides, when controlling the sequence of ideas is most important
- A list of desired future action items on which you want to focus special attention

Even when slides are necessary, make sure that *you* remain the star. One important guideline is to balance the ratio of slide time to SE time. In other words, use the slides just enough to support your ideas without detracting from your personal value.

Here are three simple and effective ideas to help you achieve this goal:

1. Use very brief phrases rather than complete sentences for your bullet points
What happens when you have a bullet point that is a complete sentence? The audience reads it. And what happens when you have a whole slide consisting of complete sentences? They read the whole slide and pay little attention to you. Go through your slides and edit down complete sentences into a few, key, intriguing words. This will *force* you to elaborate on the points, keeping the audience's attention where it belongs - on you.

There are exceptions to this rule. Examples of when you should use complete sentences for bullet points include; summary slides, quotes, requests for specific actions and technology that requires verbatim formatting.

Here are a few examples of proper and improper bullet point construction. Notice how each of the *Excellent* examples require elaboration on the part of the SE:

Poor:
- *Standards based software makes it easy to integrate new programs into your system.*

Excellent:
- *Standards = Integration ease*

Poor:
- *Field Sales needs better information from Manufacturing to estimate delivery dates for their clients.*

Excellent:
- *Field Sales information needs*

Poor:
- *Application development time will be cut down up to 20% depending on the experience of your team and how much of their day can be devoted to learning the new system and how it differs from what is currently installed.*

Excellent:
- *Application development benefits*

2. Blank out the screen

This is the most effective way I have found to instantly appear as a polished, professional presenter—and it's the easiest!

Picture yourself presenting to a client team. Behind you is a slide that contains five bullet points detailing your competitive advantages. Let's say that the first point is, *Ease of Use*. You are standing off to the side to avoid blocking the screen, in the semi-dark, when you tell the group that ease of use is one of your advantages. You would like to spend about one minute describing why ease of use is one the bullet points.

But instead of standing in the shadows, with the distraction of a bright slide behind you, you blank out the screen and step into the middle of the room. You elaborate on the point, making eye contact with all audience members. They are fully focused on you and it's clear from their reaction that you've garnered their attention and persuasively made your point. You then return to your original position, bring up the next bullet point and continue your presentation. Well done!

Presentation software may vary in how this is accomplished but I will use PowerPoint for my example. When in show mode, press the "B" key and the screen will go black.[1] Press any other key and your slide will reappear. If you would like some light on you but want the slide to disappear, press the "W" key and the screen will go white. If your reaction is, *"I can't believe I didn't know that,"* you are not alone. For whatever reason, we are consistently surprised by how many SEs don't know how to blank out the screen. If you did know about the "B" key, let this serve as a reminder of how impactful this simple technique can be.

With all presentation techniques, it is important to know when and how often to use them. Tools, like blanking out the screen, should be used sparingly. Blanking out the screen to elaborate on every bullet point, for example, would quickly irritate any audience and detract from your message.

For maximum effectiveness, blank out the screen when you:

· **Introduce yourself**

Have your introduction slide on when the audience is arriving. Then blank out the screen when you introduce yourself. Step into the middle of the room, give your introduction and then step back to your computer and bring up your next slide. This will begin the presentation on a friendly, collaborative note and help you appear to be a comfortable, confident presenter.

· **Give a lengthy elaboration**

As you discovered in the earlier example, when you wish to elaborate at length about one of your bullet points, blank out the screen to increase the audience's focus on what you are saying vs. what is on the slide behind you. This sends the message that you consider the point of particularly high importance and would appreciate the audience's serious consideration.

· **Ask the audience an open-ended question**

One technique for keeping a presentation interactive and interesting is to ask the audience questions that require lengthy responses. With the screen blanked out, the group will know that you are expecting them to respond in a meaningful way and that you have allotted time for this activity.

· End the presentation

It is important to make a personal connection with your audience at the end of your presentation. By blanking out the screen and speaking directly to your audience, you will leave a strong, intimate and honest impression. In addition, the last statement you deliver will likely be the one the audience remembers the most, so increase its impact by having the group focus 100% on you, not your slides.

Example

(with screen blanked out):

"As you've all seen today, we're very excited about providing you with a live demonstration. We have proven success in your industry and hope we get the chance to show you how our approach can help you achieve your integration goals. Thank you again and now let's open up the floor to your questions."

At the end of your next presentation try delivering this type of concluding statement, standing in the middle of the room, with the screen blanked out. You will find the effect to be quite powerful and dramatic.

3. Prepare audience questions in advance using "cheat notes"

Involving the audience by asking questions will obviously help keep you the star. The dilemma, however, is implicit in this question:

When the heat is on...

What are the chances of you remembering to ask the perfect, open-ended question, at exactly the right moment, in the middle of an, "Oh, my gosh, I can't believe the CIO just showed up," high pressure, all or nothing presentation, with your manager sitting in the back of the room?

The chances are probably pretty low. Between focusing on presenting your materials accurately, being persuasive with your delivery, answering audience questions and, in general, dealing with the pressures of such a situation, it is extremely difficult to remember to ask the perfect questions at the perfect times.

Part of my philosophy regarding presenting is simply to...

Do anything you can to minimize the pressure.

One way to minimize the pressure of remembering what questions to ask and when to ask them is to use what we refer to as *"cheat notes"* on your slides.

Although the name sounds insidious, slide cheat notes are quite legal, very moral and extremely beneficial for the presenter. Slide cheat notes are:

- Located in the bottom right hand corner of the slide
- In a font large enough for you to read but difficult for the audience to read
- In italics, making it even more difficult for the audience to read

- One key word that will easily remind you of the question you would like to ask
- Neutral enough that, if read by the audience, will not distract attention from the slide or your presentation (avoid words like *irritate*, *fail*, *warning*, etc.)

For example, here is a question that you might want to remember to ask your audience:

"How do you think the rest of the team feels about a Proof of Concept?"

Notice on the slide example that follows how the question has been distilled down to the single note, *"PoC."* When you see this word, you will remember the full question and ask it. Also, notice the size of the cheat note in relation to the main text. If the bullet font size is 36 points then the cheat note font size will be approximately 10 points. Final font size decisions should be based on room set up, screen size and where you plan to stand.

NEXT STEPS

- Line of Business approval

- Training

- Parallel testing

- Global announcement

PoC

You can see how cheat notes make it easy to talk through your bullet points and then transition to interacting with the audience. You have removed all pressure to remember exactly what to ask and when to ask it.

Participants in our classes are quick to point out that presenter notes in just about any presentation software can cover this for you without the need for cheat notes. Yes, that's true. The issue I have with presenter notes is that you need to be next to your laptop to see them. If you are moving around the room to any degree there is no way to take advantage of this feature. Anything you can do to free yourself from staring at your laptop is worth considering. With cheat notes, it doesn't where you are in the room or what side of the screen you stand on, the note is always visible. I would also add that most software does not allow you to control the font size of presenter notes, again requiring you to hover over your laptop during the presentation.

Some wonder what happens if the audience notices the cheat note? First, the chances of this happening are shockingly low. On the last day of our training classes, when we are teaching the group about cheat notes, our facilitators ask participants if they had noticed the cheat notes used during the workshop. Most will say "No." Sometimes participants will say "Yes," they have noticed the notes. When asked if they found the notes distracting or bothersome, the answer is always "No." You can expect the same reactions from your clients. Assuming that you stick with neutral words and keep the font size small, cheat notes create no distraction of consequence.

If they do notice the cheat notes this can actually be turned into a huge plus for you. Tell the customer about cheat notes. Teach them how they help the presenter remember questions to ask. The customer will most likely break out in a big smile and announce, *"That's great! I'm going to try that."* Don't be surprised if the next presentation that you see your customer deliver includes cheat notes. They'll always remember that SE who gave them a great new trick for enhancing their own presentations.

****

Presentations represent a grand opportunity for SEs. Evolving SEs understand that one key to taking full advantage of these moments is to use techniques that keep the SE the star and central focal point. While slides are usually required and expected in a highly technical presentation, the techniques in this chapter will serve to reinforce your personal value and leave the client feeling grateful and appreciative that you were there to facilitate the content.

(1) In PowerPoint, the "B" key changes by language. For example, if you were using the French version of PowerPoint, the "N" key would black out the screen as the French word for black is "noir." White in French is "blanc" and therefore the "B" key would change the screen to white.

Chapter 19

SATISFY PERSONAL NEEDS

E volving SEs understand the impact of personal needs on an organization's decision process. The challenge is that personal needs are difficult to uncover and rarely articulated yet will frequently trump business needs when final decisions are made. Have you ever been involved in a sale where you clearly had superior technology at a fair price yet lost the deal? There's a good chance that a personal need for one of the key decision makers was either not uncovered or not satisfied. So, while prospects almost always contact vendors based on business needs, top-performing, evolving SEs devote significant time and attention to satisfying personal needs as well.

Typical personal needs for clients include them wanting to:
- Feel in control of the sales process
- Be perceived as technical experts
- Show their managers that they are being tough and demanding with the SE's company
- Be publicly acknowledged for their contributions

- Develop a personal relationship with the SE
- Avoid a personal relationship with the SE/just stick to business
- Feel like their company is important to the SE's company
- Feel like the SE's solution will not negatively impact job security for themselves or colleagues
- Avoid adding any responsibilities to their existing ones
- Have the SE provide knowledge transfer to increase the clients' personal value

As you can see, personal needs cover a very wide spectrum. They can be related to how the SE's product will impact the client's work life or personal life. Clients frequently have multiple personal needs that evolving SEs are keen to uncover. Questions to ponder include asking yourself if your solution will:

- *Make the client's job easier or more complex?*
- *Require longer hours to learn and integrate with existing technology?*
- *Interfere with personal commitments?*

Evolving SEs understand that even cool, detached clients have personal needs that, when met, will greatly enhance the SE's ability to persuade and succeed. Remember:

Even in a business setting, personal needs are at play.

Because of the omnipresence of these personal needs, it is important to analyze this issue for every key relationship in each of your accounts. It is wise to embed a section for personal needs analysis into all formal planning materials and discussions. Often your AMs will have excellent insight into personal client motivations and can be great resources for this data. By simply asking your AM *"What do you think the client's personal needs are in this deal?"* you are likely to acquire important information. As a side benefit, if the AM has not pondered this question, he or she will appreciate being reminded of the importance of this analysis. Devoting even a small amount of planning time to focus on personal needs will yield an extremely high return on time invested.

****

Here is an example from one of our classes that highlights the importance of understanding personal needs.

The client had called the SE's company to ask for a quote for an Enterprise software application. When Nadim, the SE assigned to the account, went to meet the Lead Manager, he wondered why they were considering a new vendor. This account had been loyal to a competitor for many years and, in fact, had refused to take calls from other vendors for as long as Nadim could remember.

The AM, Sue, had given Nadim, some good background information. Apparently, the license on the client's current agreement was going to end in about 60 days. The Lead Manager told Sue that he was interested in seeing what else was out there, although he revealed no compelling business reason to change. So, while Sue was thrilled to get a shot at the business, she did not see a high potential for this deal to come through. Maybe the Lead Manager was just performing his due diligence or wanted to use Sue's company to put price pressure on the existing provider. If this was true, she expected it would turn into a price war, so she warned Nadim not to mention pricing or allude to the fact that there was room for some discount on this product.

With this information in hand, Nadim met with the Lead Manager. After establishing rapport and asking some initial technical questions, he realized that the business needs were quite generic and, in fact, by the end of the second meeting it was clear that the entrenched competitor had covered all the bases pretty well. Since any further discussion of the client's business needs felt like a dead end, during the third meeting Nadim decided to focus on personal needs and see what he might uncover.

Not surprisingly, Nadim did not have to work hard at this because he had planned a series of thought-provoking questions (see Chapter 12) that focused on the personal needs of the client.

Nadim:
"We've never worked together before, so I'm curious, what is important to you in terms of the relationship you like to maintain with your software partners?"

Lead Manager (smirking):
"I can tell you one thing. Don't tell me that you have a really big client who is upset and you need to take care of them right away. My company's money is as good as anyone else's. I understand that you can't always take care of me first and we

*may not be your biggest customer, but **if I ever hear that again** from a vendor, I will stop doing business with them."*

Nadim:

"I appreciate your candor. You're right, we can't always take care of everyone first but every client is equally as important as the next and you'll be treated that way. If that ever feels like an issue when working with us, please let Sue and I know because I'm certain that we're on the same page when it comes to this issue."

Nadim then told Sue about the exchange. Obviously, respect and being treated as important as everyone else were the personal needs that the current vendor had marginalized. They decided to arrange an executive visit by the regional VP to the client's site to further instill how important the client and this deal were to their company.

Nadim, Sue and the VP visited the client the next week and it was a complete success. The client wore a suit, not the very casual clothes he had on before and had cleaned up his office considerably. He also conspicuously displayed awards he had received from his company for design excellence. There was a clock on his desk, that was not there before, from the IEEE Engineering Society thanking him for a speech he had recently given to the association. The Lead Manager repeated his need for respect to the VP and shared other strategic information that was new to Sue. The meeting ended on a positive, highly collaborative note.

Sue and Nadim told the Lead Manager of an initiative their company had established that focused on building customer loyalty. It was called the *Very Important*

Customer Declaration of Commitments, and included a plaque given to each client, detailing the treatment they would receive and the commitments they would enjoy as a customer. Sure, it was a marketing tool, but it still reinforced the importance that Sue and Nadim's company placed on client relationships. These commitments were not based on purchase volume or any other criteria. All customers received the declaration and were entitled to its benefits.

Apparently the client was more fed-up with his current vendor (and impressed with Sue and Nadim) than anticipated. Sue and Nadim won the business and, while there was some back and forth on price, the final margin was excellent. Sue had the VP call the customer once the deal was done to thank him for his business and welcome him aboard.

The scenario's outcome could be traced directly back to Nadim's interest in discovering and addressing personal needs. His ability to uncover the real issue and communicate his findings to Sue was clearly the turning point of the sale.

✳✳

While personal needs are this chapter's theme, as an SE your first tier of attention will most always be business needs. You were brought in to focus on technical issues and you should meet this customer expectation. The opportunity to discuss personal needs is one that must be earned and usually comes later in the sales cycle.

Expect clients to be wary about revealing anything too personal until the relationship has been established. For example, when you meet a client for the first time and ask *"How was your weekend?,"* they will almost always reply politely and comfortably. But by going one step further and asking, *"What did you do?"* you risk getting too personal and evoking a defensive reaction. This is subject to a number of variables including your region's cultural norms, the client's corporate culture and individual personality preferences. So, while asking business questions and engaging in casual rapport building is expected, the right to get truly personal will require time and patience.

The personal needs discussion occurs when the client believes that:

1. **The SE's solution has a reasonable chance of solving the client's technical issues.**
2. **The SE is mature, can be confided in and trusted with information of a more personal nature.**

On the first point, clients want to be sure that you can provide the required technical solution before getting personal. Because exposing personal agendas usually carries some risk, they will feel little motivation to discuss these areas until you have proven your technical competence.

Next, they must feel that they can trust you with their personal needs. Can you keep a secret? Is there any chance that you will inappropriately share their needs with others? To meet this criterion usually requires a few interactions. One way to help instill trust is to not reveal the personal needs of others in the client's organization.

Show that you're not a gossip and that you respect every-one's privacy equally.

Once you have satisfied **both** of the above, the stage is set for a personal needs discussion. Clients may directly state their personal needs, *"I don't want to take the time to learn a new process"* or more subtly drop clues, *"I guess if I have to learn a new process I will."* Either way, by being a good listener and probing for more details you should be able to gain an understanding of what personal needs are at play and strategize how to best satisfy those needs.

✱✱✱

In summary, in a technology sale it's easy to get caught up in solely focusing on business needs and miss critically important personal needs. However, with care-ful observation and a few well-timed questions you can uncover what's important on a personal level to those involved in the decision process. Top-performing SEs leverage this information and present solutions in a con-text that shows sensitivity to these personal needs, lead-ing to more meaningful and loyal relationships.

FINAL THOUGHTS

T he goal for writing *The Evolving Sales Engineer* was to provide SEs and their management teams with proven techniques and mindsets for succeeding in the field based on changing demands from clients and team members. I hope that you marked and will revisit pages that ade you nod your head, smile, or realize that you had just read an idea that had never occurred to you and made total sense.

If you are an SE, talk to your manager about what you found most relevant. He or she will appreciate your initiative and probably learn something new for his or her personal use.

If you are an SE manager, conduct mini-training sessions on some of the techniques that you found particularly interesting and believe your team would truly derive value from learning. In addition, take the initiative to identify candidates for coaching relationships to elevate the performances of those who could benefit most from such an arrangement.

The secret to long term application of the ideas in this book is simply stage time. The sooner and more frequently you try them out the quicker you will find yourself using them without requiring conscious effort. You will soon be catching yourself walking out of meetings, realizing, *"Hey, I did a great job handling that objection"* or *"I really teed up the conversation well."* In time, these techniques will become a natural part of what defines you as an SE.

In conclusion, the price of admission for succeeding as an SE has changed forever. I hope this book has provided you with ideas for pursuing your quest to be perceived as a technical expert *plus* a consultative and trusted advisor. As an evolving SE you will find your services in high demand, with new doors opening and grand opportunities surfacing. As an SE manager, by encouraging and nurturing this evolution, you will be delightfully surprised and impressed by your team's ability to exceed team and client expectations as waves of change in the business world continue to wash up on your shores.

INDEX